ANALYZING THE CHINESE MILITARY

A REVIEW ESSAY AND RESOURCE GUIDE ON THE PEOPLE'S LIBERATION ARMY

PETER MATTIS
The Jamestown Foundation

To Mai and Sophie
Who provided much-needed motivation

Copyright © 2015 Peter Mattis

All rights reserved. No portion of this book may be reproduced in any fashion, print, facsimile, or electronic, or by any method yet to be developed, without the express written permission of the author.

Cover image from a U.S. Department of Defense photo taken during Secretary of Defense Robert Gates' January 2011 visit to China by U.S. Air Force Master Sgt. Jerry Morrison in the public domain.

ISBN-13: 978-1511952224

Table of Contents

Introduction	1
Building Blocks for Analyzing the PLA and Chinese Sources	7
The Annual PLA Conference	22
Chinese Security Conferences for the Advanced Reader	37
The PLA's Industrial Backbone	47
Propaganda and Political Warfare	57
Strategic Asia and the China Challenge	64
Conclusion and Takeaways	72
Appendixes	
1. Sources for China-Related Analysis	79
2. Understanding China	83
3. Analyzing Foreign Militaries	85
4. Key Concepts and Phrases	86
5. The PLA Watchers	92
6. Select PLA and Chinese Security Bibliography	96
7. The 1990s Revolution in the PLA	118
8. The PLA and the Party	119
9. Chinese Government Documents	120
10. Core Chinese-Language Readings	123
11. Works Reviewed (In Order)	126
Index	128
Acknowledgements	141
About the Author	141

INTRODUCTION

As China has risen to international prominence, two trends have increased the amount of China work performed and published by non-specialists. First, the number of people with a strong China background remains insufficient to handle all of the China-related work and thinking that needs to be completed in the intelligence, foreign policy, and defense establishments. There is little reason to think that this deficiency can be solved, even though Asian studies programs at policy-oriented schools have expanded, like Georgetown, and new opportunities have appeared, like the Master's degree at the Hopkins-Nanjing Center and Chinese-language events put on by the American Mandarin Society. Moreover, the complete domination of China-related work by China specialists would not necessarily be a good thing, because every discipline requires fresh air and fresh thinking.

Second, China has become a hot topic, attracting attention from all quarters and expanding both the demand for and supply of analysis of Chinese affairs. Writing is one of the most important ways that people think through issues and their implications. This very human inclination to commit thoughts to paper—and to distinguish oneself through writing—often produces articles without an informed understanding of how to assess Chinese sources of wildly disparate reliability. The China-watching community often takes the understandable but unfortunate position that it needs to "clean up" the mistakes and act as gatekeepers in reaction to the outpouring of non-specialist analysis. Yet, the methods and standards for how to analyze China are not very transparent to those who are not professional sinologists. The situation is made more difficult by the fact that part of China's official and nonofficial commentary on foreign and national security policy is intended to shape perceptions abroad and encourage nationalist sentiment at home. Only a few published articles and books by seasoned Western China experts explicitly describe the techniques and epistemology of analyzing China, leaving the aspiring generalist without much effective guidance.

[1]

INTRODUCTION

This review essay aims to help provide a bridge between recently-published specialist literature on the People's Liberation Army (PLA) and the generalist, technical specialist, or student, who by interest or position is trying to address the implications of China's military modernization. China's rise, the PLA, and how national security professionals should approach the questions raised by these two developments are too important to be left within a specialized research community. If war is too important to be left to the generals, then China is too important to be left to the "China Hands." But if the China-watching community should be more welcoming, then the generalists also should have a better appreciation of the difficulties of analyzing China, especially in the security realm, and aspire to a greater level of competence in evaluating sources and deriving meaning from China's burgeoning growth of open source materials. The wall of secrecy and deception that Beijing places between foreign observers and China's true state of affairs will not be bridged by a flash of insight, but rather by patient and diligent effort.

Even among the professional China analysts, substantial disagreements exist over how to evaluate China, what constitutes credible evidence, and what the key indicators are of China's trajectory.[1] When generalists and novices ignore these internal debates within the China-watching community or jump to conclusions with only a shallow appreciation of why these concerns matter, China analysts somewhat justifiably bristle with indignation. One of the few places where this conversation has taken place explicitly is CIA's professional journal *Studies in Intelligence*. Although the authors do not always engage openly with their intellectual adversaries, they

---

[1] For two such examples, see, Michael Glosny, Phillip Saunders, and Robert Ross, "Correspondence: Debating China's Naval Nationalism," *International Security*, Vol. 35, No. 2 (Fall 2010), 161–175, as well as the following exchange in *The National Interest*, Lyle Goldstein, "How China Sees America's Moves in Asia: Worse than Containment," *The National Interest*, October 29, 2014; Michael S. Chase, Timothy Heath, and Ely Ratner, "Engagement and Assurance: Debating the U.S.-China Relationship," *The National Interest*, November 5, 2014; and Lyle Goldstein, "The Great Debate: U.S.-Chinese Relations and the Future of Asia," *The National Interest*, November 10, 2014.

INTRODUCTION

do address what they think are the most important issues in analyzing China's politics at their time.[2]

However, China specialists, like members of all such specialist communities, easily slip into the mindset that their internal disputes are necessarily significant. The tendency toward parochialism leads to analysis that might miss the larger picture or overemphasize the uniqueness of Chinese approaches. Unchecked parochialism leads to myopia, especially the fallacy that more research into Chinese sources will provide the answer. The influx of new analysts and experienced generalists as well as insights from broader historical reading are indispensable for the field. They generate new questions and help refocus attention on old but still important issues.

The books and studies reviewed and evaluated in this essay were selected for their relevance to non-specialists and to build their awareness of the existing China literature, where credible analysis is being produced, and where credible sources of information are to be found. If this essay seems overly complementary to the surveyed materials, this is deliberate. The point is to highlight good habits in sourcing and analysis. This essay serves to highlight elements of a sound baseline for understanding the PLA and writing on Chinese security policy by discussing some of the analytic methods, key works, and the most reliable analysts as well as important conferences that set the agenda of Chinese security studies. Organizational

---

[2] Josh Kerbel, "Thinking Straight: Cognitive Bias in the U.S. Debate about China," *Studies in Intelligence*, Vol. 48, No. 3 (2004) <https://www.cia.gov/library/center-for-the-study-of-intelligence/kent-csi/vol48no3/html/v48i3a03p.htm>; Anonymous, "Hu's a Reformist, Hu's a Conservative: The Haos and Huais of Chinese Political Analysis," *Studies in Intelligence*, Vol. 31, No. 4 (Winter 1987) [PDF]
<http://www.foia.cia.gov/sites/default/files/DOC_0000620553.pdf >; Gail Solin, "The Art of China-Watching," *Studies in Intelligence*, Vol. 19, No. 1 (Spring 1975)
<https://www.cia.gov/library/center-for-the-study-of-intelligence/kent-csi/vol19no1/html/v19i1a04p_0001.htm>; John Dockham, "A Sharp Look at Sinosovietology," *Studies in Intelligence*, Vol. 5, No. 3 (Summer 1961) [PDF]
<https://www.cia.gov/library/center-for-the-study-of-intelligence/kent-csi/vol5no3/pdf/v05i3a09p.pdf>.

INTRODUCTION

charts and order of battle resources are highlighted for the reader's reference, wherever such research appears to have lasting value.[3]

The works surveyed here, however, will fail to equip any would-be analyst of the PLA with one important tool: a sense of organizational history. Unlike most modern militaries, the PLA did not begin with a nation-state but rather a political party engaged in an underground struggle. Today, the PLA is still the armed wing of the party, not the army of the government of the People's Republic of China—and advocating for the latter is the simplest way for an officer to be dismissed. The party also has attempted to dominate the military to ensure, in Mao Zedong's words, "that the party commands the gun, and the gun must never be allowed to command the party." Particularly under Mao and Deng Xiaoping, the leadership used their control over the PLA to push economic and other domestic policy at the expense of fighting effectiveness. The lingering peculiarities of the PLA have much to do with this history, and scholars like Ellis Joffe, Harlan Jencks, Harvey Nelsen, and William Whitson pioneered an appreciation of how the party-army relationship affects the PLA's organization and operations (See Appendix 8).

Important though it may be to develop familiarity with existing analysis, would-be writers should remember that there is no substitute for using Chinese sources. Even the English-language versions of *PLA Daily* articles and Xinhua News Agency reports offer important updates to order of battle, equipment, and policy. The PLA is evolving rapidly and tinkering constantly with its units, so even the best open source studies get overtaken by events. To help reduce the research burden, analysts can begin with sources like *The Chinese Army Today*, *The Great Wall at Sea*, or *Chinese*

---

[3] This organizational data should be used to supplement the broader, service-specific organizational details provided by the following baseline sources: Dennis J. Blasko, *The Chinese Army Today: Tradition and Transformation for the 21st Century*, 2nd Edition (New York: Routledge, 2012); *China's Navy 2007* (Washington, DC: Office of Naval Intelligence, 2007); James Mulvenon and Andrew N.D. Yang, eds., *The People's Liberation Army as Organization: Reference Volume 1.0* (Santa Monica, CA: RAND, 2002); *People's Liberation Army Air Force 2010* (Wright-Patterson AFB, OH: National Air and Space Intelligence Center, 2010). A forthcoming book will be indispensable, see, Kevin Pollpeter and Kenneth Allen, eds., *PLA as Organization v2.0* (Vienna, VA: Defense Group Inc., Forthcoming 2015).

INTRODUCTION

Aerospace Power, supplement them with annually updated resources such as the International Institute for Strategic Studies' *The Military Balance*, and then go to Chinese sources. A surprising number of Chinese military concepts also are explained for foreigners in the biannual defense white papers. Before dismissing English-language Chinese sources as pure propaganda, analysts should remember that one of the purposes of propaganda is to inform. At minimum, Beijing's interest in deterring the United States and other powers on China's periphery gives the PLA incentive to explain what it does and why with some degree of truthfulness, even if capabilities remain mysterious.

Lastly, a brief note outlining the scope of this analysis is required, because of the recent work omitted here. This guide is primarily concerned with empirical studies of the People's Liberation Army itself, not Chinese national security and foreign policy. Thoughtful scholars, like Thomas Christensen, Taylor Fravel, Alistair Iain Johnston, Oriana Skylar Mastro, and many more, have written excellent monographs and articles (some of which are provided in the appendixes) on these topics that do concern the PLA and its capabilities. Because their focus often is on Chinese policymaking rather than PLA itself, they are omitted from this essay. Those writings, nevertheless, are fundamental to an understanding of Chinese security affairs and the implications of China's rise.

To supplement the necessarily limited scope of this narrative, ten appendixes are provided to guide the reader toward additional sources of information and analysis.

- Appendix 1 provides a select, annotated list of places to go regularly for high-quality analysis of the PLA and Chinese security affairs.

- Appendix 2 is a short list of general China and U.S.-China relations books—along with easy-reading alternatives—that will help explain China's politics, trajectory, and challenges.

- Appendix 3 provides a short list of readings that are pertinent to observing and evaluating foreign militaries.

- Appendix 4 offers a brief explanation of a few key PLA concepts and phrases with which any analyst of the PLA should be familiar.

INTRODUCTION

- Appendix 5 provides a select list of analysts and scholars (with their affiliations) who routinely write about the PLA and Chinese security affairs.

- Appendix 6 provides a selected list of key books, articles, and reports that should be consulted. This appendix is organized thematically under the following headings: Background Texts on National Security and Foreign Policymaking; The People's Liberation Army - General; Organizational Basics; The PLA Ground Forces; The PLA Air Force; The PLA Navy; China's Rocket Forces: The Second Artillery; Chinese Nuclear Forces; Civil-Military Relations; China's Defense-Industrial Base; China-Taiwan Military Balance; Chinese Cyber, Information Operations, and Intelligence; China Space Issues and Space-Based Capabilities; complete listings for the conference volumes; and Congressional Research Service reports.

- Appendix 7 identifies sources that explore key developments in the 1990s affecting how the PLA has developed.

- Appendix 8 offers a few books on the historical development of the PLA and why it looks the way it looks today.

- Appendix 9 provides links to key Chinese government documents of relevance, including the defense white papers.

- Appendix 10 provides a short guide to looking for Chinese-language materials based on one's particular interests in the PLA.

- The final appendix is a list of the works reviewed.

I hope you find this book a useful introduction and guide to the People's Liberation Army and to the burgeoning literature evaluating its modernization. Understanding the Chinese military is a challenging yet engaging task, made all the more necessary by China's expanding role in international affairs.

BUILDING BLOCKS FOR ANALYZING THE PLA AND CHINESE SOURCES

- Dennis J. Blasko, *The Chinese Army Today: Tradition and Transformation for the 21st Century*, 2nd Edition (New York: Routledge, 2012).

- Paul H.B. Godwin and Alice L. Miller, *China's Forbearance Has Limits: Chinese Threat and Retaliation Signaling and Its Implications for a Sino-American Military Confrontation*, China Strategic Perspectives, No. 6 (Washington, DC: National Defense University Institute for National Strategic Studies, 2013).

- Bernard D. Cole, *The Great Wall at Sea: China's Navy Enters the Twenty-First Century*, 2nd Edition (Annapolis, MD: Naval Institute Press, 2012).

- Kevin Pollpeter and Kenneth W. Allen, eds., *PLA as Organization v2.0* (Vienna, VA: Defense Group Inc., Forthcoming 2015).

One of the most important books ever published on Chinese military affairs must be Dennis Blasko's *The Chinese Army Today: Tradition and Transformation for the 21st Century* for its structured way of explaining the PLA from the ground up. A great many of the published works on the PLA now make at least one of two assumptions about the reader. The first is that the reader is uninterested in the nuts-and-bolts of the PLA; an assumption that is unwarranted for national security professionals reading into a China account. Operational positions often require detailed knowledge of how things work, and that level of detail is hard to find outside of the office. The second assumption that is often made—most notably in some of the works surveyed below—is that the reader already is generally familiar with the PLA with respect to its organization, personnel, and capabilities. Blasko, a former assistant army attaché with tours in Beijing and Hong Kong, avoids making these two assumptions. He writes in the preface that the book "is

[7]

intended to be a baseline document for further study on the Chinese military by students, journalists, and analysts in and out of government. It is the kind of book I would have liked to have read before becoming a U.S. Army attaché to China in 1992" (p. xvii). Consequently, the book is a well-organized, detail-oriented, and comprehensive evaluation of the PLA, primarily the ground forces. It is an indispensable handbook for novices on China and even experts will find Blasko's book useful to have at hand for those little details, such as the identification features of military uniforms and PLA unit locations.

The chapters "Who is the PLA?" (pp. 56–79), "Where is the PLA?" (pp. 80–114), and "What Equipment Does the PLA Use?" (pp. 148–174) provide the basic facts about the PLA.[4] They also give a good sense of how the PLA is based and deployed within China as well as how the organization fits together. The chapters "How Will the PLA Fight?" (pp. 115–147) and "How Does the PLA Train?" (pp. 175–210) systematically explore the PLA's aspirations and how successful the PLA is at preparing itself to fight as it thinks it should. The "How Will the PLA?" chapter walks the reader through key tenets of Chinese military thought, moving beyond axiomatic treatment of Sun Tzu's *The Art of War* and Mao Zedong's military thought. More importantly, Blasko works through the *Science of Military Strategy* (*zhanlüe xue*, 战略学) and *The Science of Campaigns* (*zhanyi xue*, 战役学). These latter two works are the most authoritative recent PLA publications establishing how the Chinese military thinks about linking political ends with military means and the different kinds of campaigns/operations (e.g. joint blockade, maritime interdiction, stability maintenance, information operations, etc.) in which the PLA anticipates playing a role.

As befitting a former assistant army attaché, Blasko also devotes time to sketching out the uncertainties associated with China's rapid military modernization program. The familiar Washington refrain that Beijing is not

---

[4] Blasko's description primarily focuses on the PLA ground forces. For comparable information on the PLA Navy and PLA Air Force, see, *China's Navy 2007* (Washington, DC: Office of Naval Intelligence, 2007); *People's Liberation Army Air Force 2010* (Wright-Patterson AFB, OH: National Air and Space Intelligence Center, 2010).

transparent about PLA development obscures just how much information is available from Chinese-language sources—Blasko's endnotes for *The Chinese Army Today* run more than 40 pages. Yet there are gaps in what the PLA publicizes and even what is published contains traps for the unwary. As the book moves systematically through the PLA, the author takes care to highlight these areas, such as the PLA budget (pp. 10–13), where PLA aspirations fall short of its capabilities (pp. 137–138),[5] and how to read newspaper reports of military exercises (pp. 209–210).

If there is one criticism that can be fairly leveled at Blasko's work, it would be his tendency to summarize and not always provide hard-hitting analysis of his own. The systematic and organized presentation of how the Chinese military writes about itself and its objectives, however, has lasting value precisely because Blasko is circumspect and has let the PLA speak for itself. *The Chinese Army Today* is a reliable benchmark and a guide. In sum, *The Chinese Army Today* should be treated as one of the fundamental building blocks for preparing analysts to evaluate the PLA on its own terms—a familiar refrain from Dennis Blasko who has made a compelling case repeatedly for how different the PLA may be from its contemporary U.S. counterparts and even the Soviet-era Red Army (pp. 228–229).[6] Familiarity with the information collected in this volume allows the intrepid analyst to move forward with greater awareness of the perils in assessing the PLA as well as some of the key dynamics of China's military modernization.

In addition to the virtues of Blasko's work described above, the attention he lavishes on *The Science of Military Strategy* (*zhanlüe xue*, 战略学) and *The Science of Campaigns* (*zhanyi xue*, 战役学) should spur awareness of key PLA texts that, to the best of our knowledge, guide Chinese military thinking. Unfortunately, only the first has an English-language edition. One

---

[5] Blasko draws attention here to the critical judgment about PLA capabilities issued by the Central Military Commission, called the "Two Incompatibles" (*liang ge buxiang shiying*, 两个不相适应), which described the PLA as unable to the fulfill the core tasks given it (for more, see pages 32 and 87–88).

[6] For example, Dennis J. Blasko, "China in 2012: Shifting Perspectives - Assessing the PLA from the Ground Up," *Jamestown Foundation China Brief*, Vol. 12, No. 2, January 20, 2012.

of the mistakes most often made in generalist analysis is the reliance on *Unrestricted Warfare* (*chaoxian zhan*, 超限战) by Qiao Liang and Wang Xiangsui.[7] This provocative book attracted a lot of attention, because the authors were PLA colonels and it endorsed a comprehensive range of measures to undermine the U.S. position internationally including information and economic warfare as well as terrorism.[8] Additionally, the book was translated into English, making it easily accessible for someone without Chinese language ability and removing the need to go bookstore hopping in Beijing. The emphasis on *Unrestricted Warfare* over *The Science of Military Strategy* highlights a fundamental misunderstanding about the levels of authority in PLA publications and what the PLA publishes on national security, strategy, and related foreign policy issues.

The first thing generalists need to understand is that the PLA has a near monopoly on defense writing within the People's Republic of China (PRC), including in newspapers, magazines, journals, and books. The volume is overwhelming, but not everything is a statement of policy or representative of PLA thinking. Every professional military needs to exchange ideas to communicate thinking across units and geographic barriers as well as to spur creative thinking about the challenges of modern warfare in a time of rapid technological change. For books, individual authorship, like in *Unrestricted Warfare*, is a sign that the authors alone are responsible for the contents, almost irrespective of the publisher and the author(s)'s rank and position. In the pursuit of more authoritative sources, readers should look

---

[7] The FBIS translation of Qiao Liang and Wang Xiangsui, *Unrestricted Warfare* (Beijing: PLA Arts and Literature Publishing House, 1999) is freely available online <http://www.cryptome.org/cuw.htm>.

[8] Since that time, the PLA has continued thinking about and developing capabilities covered in *Unrestricted Warfare*, especially cyber, electronic warfare, and information operations (or perception management). The influence of this book, however, in generating those capabilities remains unknown, particularly because senior operational commanders began developing similar ideas and who, because of their position, were capable of implementing them, such as Dai Qingmin who led the PLA's electronic warfare department. For a favorable review in retrospect, see, Larry M. Wortzel, *The Dragon Extends Its Reach: Chinese Military Power Goes Global* (Herndon, VA: Potomac Books Inc., 2013).

for books with multiple *editors*, vice authors, and background comments identifying which departments coordinated on the publication.

Compared to Qiao and Liang's uncoordinated musings in *Unrestricted Warfare*, *The Science of Military Strategy* (2001 edition) has two principle editors, Peng Guangqian and Yao Yuzhi, as well as 35 other contributors from the PLA's Academy of Military Science.[9] This organization is the highest-level military research organization, which produces and coordinates research on national security, armed forces development, and operations for the PLA as well as the Central Military Commission (CMC).[10] Moreover, *The Science of Military Strategy* was coordinated with a number of important PLA departments, including the General Staff Department. In 2013, the Academy of Military Science released a new edition penned by unidentified members of the academy's Strategic Research Department. This edition, however, might be less authoritative, because its coordination did not include as many critical PLA departments as the 2001 edition.[11]

The issue of authoritativeness in Chinese publications and sources is something that cannot be taken for granted, despite the presumed level of control the authorities exercise over what gets published related to Chinese capabilities and intentions. Intelligence officers and all others responsible for Indicators and Warning (I&W) will applaud a recent study published by the U.S. National Defense University's Institute for National Strategic Studies: *China's Forbearance Has Limits: Chinese Threat and Retaliation Signaling and Its Implications for a Sino-American Military Confrontation*. Written by two veteran China analysts, Paul Godwin and Alice Miller provide a systematic review of Beijing's attempts to signal intentions prior to using military force.

---

[9] An English-language translation of this edition became available in 2005, see, Peng Guangqian and Yao Youzhi, eds., *The Science of Military Strategy* (Beijing: Military Science Publishing House, 2005).

[10] Bates Gill and James Mulvenon, "China's Military-Related Think Tanks and Research Institutions," *The China Quarterly*, No. 171 (2002), 622–623.

[11] For thorough discussion of how *The Science of Military Strategy* has evolved, see, Joe McReynolds, ed., *China's Evolving Military Strategy* (Washington, DC: The Jamestown Foundation, Forthcoming 2015).

The value of this study, however, goes well beyond its immediate topic, because the authors provide one of the few explicit descriptions of the hierarchy of Chinese publications and what they represent (pp. 30–34).

Godwin and Miller assess three kinds of Chinese statements: leadership, Ministry of Foreign Affairs (MFA), and the *People's Daily*. Leadership statements are the easiest to evaluate, because the level of authoritativeness follows rank. Authoritative statements of policy only appear from the party general secretary (head of state) and the premier of the State Council (head of government). At steadily degrading levels, these are followed by statements from members of the Political Bureau (Politburo) of the party's Central Committee and vice premiers of the State Council, the members of the Central Committee, and, finally, provincial party secretaries. The MFA statements proceed in descending order: statements of the PRC government (e.g. Beijing's announcement of the East China Sea Air Defense Identification Zone in November 2013), statements of the Ministry of Foreign Affairs, statements from the MFA spokesman, and comments from the daily MFA press briefing.

Evaluating Chinese newspapers is substantially tougher, because institutionally-supported media have been supplemented by a rapidly growing commercial media sector. Many of the principal Chinese newspapers are the official outlets for important institutions. The *People's Daily* is the mouthpiece of the party's Central Committee; Xinhua of the State Council. The PLA, the Ministry of Public Security, the United Front Work Department, Central Party School, and others all have their media outlets. These newspapers may represent the institution, but, apart from the *People's Daily*, they cannot provide authoritative statements of government policy and intent. Similar to PLA books, anonymity rather than individuality is the sign of authority. At top of the hierarchy for identifying institutional views is the unsigned editorial without any acknowledged authorship. Anything else, according to Godwin and Miller, qualifies as "quasi-authoritative," such as commentator (*pinglunyuan*, 评论员) and observer articles, as well as pseudonymous articles from the likes of Zhong Sheng (钟声, a homophone for "Voice of China"). Signed editorials require an assessment of the author, and their authoritativeness derives from the author's position.

Commercial papers, like the oft-provocative *Global Times*, now draw a lot of foreign attention for their nationalistic and fiery op-eds as well as derisive (even humorous) commentary on foreign discourse related to China. Although these media outlets have a parent organization—for example, the *Global Times* is part of the media group publishing the *People's Daily*—they are commercial in nature and do not represent institutional views.[12] They are, however, used for propaganda aimed primarily at domestic audiences and must operate within the official guidelines.

The hierarchies identified by Godwin and Miller provide a framework for the China novice to evaluate their sources. The practical application of this framework is visible throughout the works that will be reviewed below. Checking the citations, readers will note the best analysts of the PLA do not draw on the commercial press, but focus their energy on the PLA's official outlets as well as the papers of the PLA's three services and one independent branch: the ground forces, the PLA Navy, the PLA Air Force, and the Second Artillery. Similarly, these analysts also evaluate the authorship and organizational affiliation. War-fighting, strategy, and intentions are the province of senior officers in places like the Central Military Commission, the four general departments (known in Chinese as the *si zongbu* [四总部]; General Staff, Logistics, Political, and Armaments[13]), service headquarters departments, and the military regions as well as the Academy of Military Science and the National Defense University.

---

[12] For a thorough examination of the media environment in China and its implications, including military journalism, see, Susan Shirk, ed., *Changing Media, Changing China* (New York: Oxford University Press, 2011). For a summary version, see David Bandurski, "How the Southern Weekly Protests Moved the Bar on Press Control," *Jamestown Foundation China Brief*, Vol. 13, No. 3, February 1, 2013.

[13] For a detailed description of these departments, see, respectively in Mulvenon and Yang, eds., *The PLA as Organization 1.0*, David Finkelstein, "The General Staff Department of the Chinese People's Liberation Army: Organization, Roles, and Mission," 122–224; Susan Puska, "The People's Liberation Army (PLA) General Logistics Department: Toward Joint Logistics Support," 247–272; Larry Wortzel, "The General Political Department and the Evolution of the Political Commissar System," 225–246; and Harlan Jencks, "The General Armament Department," 273–308.

Failing to understand these general guidelines is the fastest way for well-intentioned generalists to fall afoul of the specialist China-watching community. This seems a daunting task for the amateur China watcher and generalist first approaching the PLA, and one that encourages devotion to Chinese-language study. Language skills, however, are only one part of the skill set required to evaluate the PLA, and experience and functional expertise (e.g. logistics, aviation, and surface warfare operations) contribute positively to the study of the Chinese military. Nowhere is this better proved than Bernard "Bud" Cole's work on the PLA Navy, including the second edition of *The Great Wall at Sea: China's Navy Enters the Twenty-First Century*. Cole is a retired U.S. Navy Captain with a Ph.D. in history, currently affiliated with the U.S. National War College. For many years, he has analyzed Chinese naval capabilities and developments at the strategic and tactical levels with impressive authority.

The book sets the stage for examining current Chinese naval capabilities by exploring the PLAN's naval heritage and China's growing set of interests, both maritime and economic. From almost the beginning of the People's Republic, naval forces—perhaps better described in their early years as coastal defense forces—have played a vital role in protecting Chinese national security. The PLAN began as no more than a few patrol craft as well as a handful of aging Soviet destroyers and submarines, but Beijing almost immediately put them to use beginning with the successful attack and occupation of Hainan Island in 1950. Cole quickly summarizes several stages of the PLAN's slow but steady development into a more serious navy as well as its actions in the Taiwan Strait (1950, 1954–1955, 1958) and the South China Sea (1974, 1988, 1995, 1998). One of the key judgments in Cole's analysis is that "Beijing's willingness to resort to naval force even when significantly outgunned bears a cautionary message for foreign strategists evaluating China's possible actions during a crisis" (p. 18).[14] This evaluation implies evaluating PLA capabilities is only the first and easiest step for assessing how China might use force and the potential

---

[14] Cole's point here is explored in detail in Mark Ryan, David Finkelstein and Michael McDevitt, eds., *Chinese Warfighting: The PLA Experience since 1949* (Armonk, NY: M.E. Sharpe, 2003).

threat Chinese military modernization poses to the current regional alignment. Somewhere at the intersection of interests and capabilities, Beijing will make choices about coercion, war, and peace. These choices are not the subject of *The Great Wall at Sea*; however, Cole has a great deal to say about how the PLAN's modernization is aligned with Chinese interests.

Beijing's interests have expanded much faster than the navy's capability to protect them, and "China today is among the nations most dependent on the oceans for food, energy, and trade" (p. 57). The expansion of China's economy, the energy needed to fuel it, intensifying maritime territorial disputes, and the fisheries ever farther afield that Chinese fishing boats chase makes Chinese leaders nervous. Cole does not go into detail on each of these interests, but does specifically identify important concerns—such as with which countries over what islands China has disputes (pp. 24–36)—that drive the PLAN developments and Chinese naval strategy.

The next chapters of the book go into the PLAN's organizational structure and equipment as well as its "ability to fulfill that responsibility" created by Chinese interests. For perspective on the Chinese navy's development, Cole offers a set of tables counting the PLAN's surface ship inventory for 1955, 1960, 1970, 1980, 1990, 2000, and 2010 (pp. 88–93).[15] The tables give an immediate sense of how rapid China's shipbuilding and purchasing have accelerated, particularly since 2000. The book introduces the PLAN's fleet system (pp. 70–76), China's division of labor for air defense (pp. 77–78), and the roles of China's coast guard (pp. 78–82). This treatment of PLAN organization lacks the detail that Blasko developed in *The Chinese Army Today*, which is a more reliable resource for explaining the ins-and-outs of organizational matters. Cole's treatment, however, benefits from conciseness without overwhelming detail.

One of the best chapters is Cole's final chapter on China's maritime strategy. At a time when a search for "Chinese strategy" yields literally thousands of articles, this chapter serves as an exemplar for how one

---

[15] For the most current inventory of PLAN ships and their fleet assignments, see, *The PLA Navy: New Capabilities and Missions for the 21st Century* (Washington, DC: Office of Naval Intelligence, 2015) <http://www.oni.navy.mil/Intelligence_Community/china.html>.

should go about analyzing strategy. It is transparent. The author explains the tenets of the approach he will use to evaluate whether China has a functioning maritime strategy. Even better, he does so on the basis of how the PLAN might judge itself and China. Cole draws from the *PLAN Encyclopedia* to identify a set of factors that shape modern naval strategy, namely: professionalization of the officer corps; naval systems; defense industry infrastructure; the ability to derive doctrine and tactics; operate tactical units beyond individual ships; intelligence production, analysis, and dissemination; service-wide strategic planning; national maritime leadership; and the effectiveness of naval strategists in national strategy-making structure (p. 170). He then uses that chapter to explore these factors and, ultimately, suggest that Beijing pursues "a maritime strategy consciously designed to achieve near term national security objectives and longer-term regional maritime dominance through both combatant and merchant fleets" (p. 187). The believability of Cole's assertion stems from his earlier analysis of Chinese interests and the development of naval capabilities as well as the structured way in which he addresses strategy.

Between Blasko, Miller and Godwin, and Cole, readers will be introduced to both good analysis and some of the fundamentals of analyzing the PLA. Although the equipment and organizational structure sections of *The Chinese Army Today* and *The Great Wall at Sea* have been slowly overtaken by events, the authors make it easy to begin building one's own databases off their reliably-built foundations. Taking full advantage of the subsequent works surveyed here depends on mastering the basics of the PLA and understanding how to evaluate Chinese sources. These are indispensable references for any China bookshelf, because they portray the PLA within the broader Chinese context and the government's political-military concerns. These works are soon to be joined a fourth critical work on understanding all aspects of the PLA and its modernization process.

The organizational dimension of Blasko and Cole's work is one of the strengths of their analysis; however, those details go out of date faster than one would like. The most comprehensive and current resource on PLA organization is the forthcoming *PLA as Organization v2.0* to be published by Defense Group Inc. (DGI). DGI's Center for Intelligence Research and Analysis, co-founded by James Mulvenon, is a defense contractor employing some of the best young analysts of Chinese security affairs. *PLA as Organization v2.0* draws upon some of those talents alongside more established experts, such as Kenneth Allen, Dennis Blasko, Dean Cheng, John Corbett, and Lonnie Henley. The book updates a conference volume that was edited by Mulvenon and produced by RAND and the Chinese Center for Advanced Policy Studies fifteen years ago.[16] The PLA has changed dramatically since that volume was published—including changes to its order of battle, new equipment, missions, and doctrine—making this new book a welcome reference.

Like its predecessor, *PLA as Organization v2.0* covers the Chinese military's principal organizations, such as the services and the four general departments, but adds the PLA's most likely wartime command structure and structure of the People's Armed Police. The editors also explicitly note that this book is intended to serve as a reference guide rather than a book to be read from cover to cover. The two most significant departures from and improvement over the original RAND volume are the disciplined inclusion of Chinese terminology for *everything* and the discussion of sources at the beginning of each organization's chapter. With the publication of this volume, there will not be a better place to go to find the formal Chinese names for nearly every organizational element throughout the PLA as well as unit names, rank and grade, and much more.

One of the volume's editors, former assistant air attaché Kenneth Allen, opens the book with a chapter explaining the overarching elements of PLA structure and function from administrative departments, party committees, and military regions. This chapter also provides a clear description of the PLA's grade system (officer ranks are primarily for engaging foreign militaries) (pp. 10–15), civilians' status within the PLA (p. 17), and how to identify PLA personnel by their uniforms (pp. 17–18). Other useful elements include a complete list of PLA educational institutions (pp. 32–39, 61–66) along with an appendix of key terminology and concepts that address the different levels of PLA structure from the CMC down to the regiment (pp. 40–50). Perhaps even more than other elements of the

---

[16] Mulvenon and Yang, eds., *The People's Liberation Army as Organization: Reference Volume 1.0.*

[17]

volume, this opening chapter is descriptive and matter-of-fact; however, it provides the basic terminology that any analyst can use for detailed Chinese-language research.

Some of the organizational details in *The PLA as Organization 2.0* can be found throughout other recent sources—such as Office of Naval Intelligence and National Air & Space Intelligence Center reports, respectively, on the PLAN and PLAAF[17]—but nowhere else can one find anything of substance on the Ministry of National Defense (MND). Four experienced authors, all current or former U.S. intelligence officials, combined their notes to investigate whether MND is a substantial organization in its own right or a shell organization for other PLA elements, or what the Chinese call "one organization with two plaques" (*yi ge jigou liang kuai paizi*, 一个机构两块牌子). The authors conclude the MND's key function is to manage relations with non-PLA organizations, both domestically and abroad, allowing the PLA to "preserve its position as a self-referential and semi-independent '*xitong*' (sub-system) within [China's] power structure" (p. 87). Despite MND's authority over military matters defined in the Chinese constitution and its once prominent position for so-called dual political-military elites like Lin Biao and Peng Dehuai to exercise influence in both the civil and military spheres, the party's Central Military Commission (CMC) actually performs the work that MND's international counterparts in "commanding and managing the military" (pp. 88–89). The authors also provide a comprehensive overview of MND's organizational structure and its overlap with offices in various parts of the PLA as well as MND's engagement with the outside world. They also conclude with a useful list of information gaps relating to the MND's role in Chinese policymaking, because, despite MND's basic hollowness, the minister's status as a CMC and a minister under the State Council places him in many policymaking and coordinating groups (pp. 105–106).

---

[17] *China's Navy 2007* (Washington, DC: Office of Naval Intelligence, 2007); *People's Liberation Army Air Force 2010* (Wright-Patterson AFB, OH: National Air and Space Intelligence Center, 2010). The most recent report from the Office of Naval Intelligence provides a current inventory of ships in the navy's three fleets; however, it lacks other organizational details present in the 2007 report, see, *The PLA Navy: New Capabilities and Missions for the 21st Century* (Washington, DC: Office of Naval Intelligence, 2015).

The next four chapters systematically address the General Staff Department (pp. 120–44), General Political Department (pp. 145–156), General Logistics Department (pp. 157–198), and the General Armament Department (pp. 199–234). If the General Political Department chapter does not offer as deep of a description of its counterpart in *The PLA as Organization v1.0* with respect explaining what the department does on a daily basis and the role of political commissars, the depth and detail of the General Armament Department (GAD) chapter more than compensates for any shortcomings. This chapter offers substantial improvement over the previous edition, because, at the time of the first conference, the GAD was newly-established (1998) and it was not clear how expansive the department's responsibilities would be.

Typical of the ground force dominance of the PLA's central organizations, the GAD focuses on ground force, nuclear, and space technology research, development, and acquisition. No officer outside the ground forces has become one of the many GAD deputy directors, and it appears the PLAN, PLAAF, and Second Artillery manage their own equipment development and acquisition (pp. 199–200). The chapter identifies the subordinate bureaus and their functions, enumerating an alphabet soup of bureaucracies that range from the mundane to the unique Science and Technology Committee (*kexue jishu weiyuanhui*, 科学技术委员会). Led by a military region leader-grade officer, this committee reports directly to the CMC, employs a wide-range of experts inside and outside the PLA, and oversees at least 51 expert groups that advise military leaders on a range of technology issues (pp. 201–202, 206–209). While, like the other chapters, ultimate judgment of GAD's effectiveness goes beyond the scope, enough material is provided for intrepid researchers to find a starting point.

The next four chapters explore the ground forces, PLAN, PLAAF, and Second Artillery. Each chapter chronicles the organizational evolution of each service, and, in the Second Artillery's case, the expansion of capability and prestige. Both the ground forces and the PLAN provide more up-to-date information than *The Chinese Army Today* and *The Great Wall at Sea*. The services section also benefits from a short chapter on the People's Armed Police, China's paramilitary force founded in the 1980s.

The final chapter, by the Heritage Foundation's Dean Cheng, addresses the PLA's probable wartime structure as identified by Chinese military writings. The chapter proceeds as PLA thinking has done, beginning with lessons learned about modern warfare being integrated into the PLA's "military theory" (*junshi lilun*, 军事理论) "and from there to its organization" (p. 414).[18] The discussion of military theory provides several key features of "local war under modern, high-technology conditions," including high operational tempo, emphasis on joint operations, and the paramount importance of command, control, communications, and intelligence for all sides of a conflict.[19] These lead to an emphasis on "key point strikes" (*zhongdian daji*, 重点打击), because the military objective is now to paralyze the enemy rather than pursue a Clausewitzian war of annihilation (p. 415). To fight this kind of war, the PLA recognizes the need for new joint campaign structures—China's previous wars were ground force-centric and barely involved the PLAAF and PLAN (pp. 416–417). What PLA officers observed from the U.S. wars in the Balkans and Iraq expanded on these themes, leading to updates of PLA doctrinal regulations on what war will look like and what will be required organizationally if China fights another war. For example, "key point strikes" became "constrain the enemy with precision strikes" (*jing da zhi di*, 精打制敌) and the PLA, at least in writing, pushed for full integration not just of forces, but also of domains and battlespaces (pp. 423–427)—a belief that also necessitates new command structures (pp. 430–435). The only comparable analysis with this kind of

---

[18] The PLA does not have "doctrine" for warfighting. For a rough comparison of Chinese and U.S. doctrinal terminology, see, David Shambaugh, "PLA Strategy and Doctrine: Recommendation for a Future Research Agenda," Paper for "Chinese Military Studies: a Conference on the State of the Field," U.S. National Defense University, Fort McNair, October 26–27, 2000 <http://www.comw.org/cmp/fulltext/0010shambaugh.htm>.

[19] This chapter is best read in conjunction with Cheng's chapter reviewed below on lessons from the two U.S. wars with Iraq, see, Dean Cheng, "Chinese Lessons from the Gulf Wars," in Andrew Scobell, David Lai, and Roy Kamphausen, eds., *Chinese Lessons from Other Peoples' War* (Carlisle, PA: Army War College Strategic Studies Institute, 2011), 153–200.

detail is the series of articles by retired Department of Defense analyst Kevin McCauley focusing on unit integration under these new concepts.[20]

Cheng's analysis is necessarily speculative, given that the precise command arrangements remain unknown. The Chinese military writings, written as they are for open consumption, focus on the underlying philosophy behind what the PLA wants to accomplish while refraining from identifying concrete organizational issues. To maintain their relevance, the authors do reference specific PLA guiding documents that have not been published in their entirety, such as "Essentials" (*gangyao*, 纲要) or "Regulations" (*tiaoling*, 条令).[21] Occasionally, summaries of these important documents can be found in the *PLA Daily* or Xinhua, and they are worth finding because they are official pronouncements about military policy rather than less authoritative analyses of military affairs.

The best use of *The PLA as Organization v2.0* is in conjunction with a good service-specific book, such as *The Chinese Army Today* or *The Great Wall at Sea*. The organizational details and Chinese-language terminology in *The PLA as Organization v2.0* combines well with the latter's empirical data on history, equipment, doctrine, and missions. For those with Chinese-language ability, many of the chapters contain appendixes or otherwise mark useful terminology. Once this volume becomes publicly available, it will belong alongside the other works in this section.

---

[20] Kevin McCauley, "The PLA's Three-Pronged Approach to Achieving Jointness in Command and Control," *Jamestown Foundation China Brief*, Vol. 12, No. 6, March 15, 2012; "Developing a Framework for PLA Precision Operations," *Jamestown Foundation China Brief*, Vol. 12, No. 13, July 6, 2012; "Systems of Systems Operational Capability: Key Supporting Concepts for Future Joint Operations," *Jamestown Foundation China Brief*, Vol. 12, No. 19, October 5, 2012; "Systems of Systems Operational Capability: Operational Units and Elements," *Jamestown Foundation China Brief*, Vol. 13, No. 6, March 15, 2013; "Systems of Systems Operational Capability: Impact on PLA Transformation," *Jamestown Foundation China Brief*, Vol. 13, No. 8, April 12, 2013.

[21] For an overview of PLA documents and their hierarchy, see, David Finkelstein, "China's National Military Strategy: An Overview of the 'Military Strategic Guidelines'," in Roy Kamphausen and Andrew Scobell, eds., *Right Sizing the People's Liberation Army: Exploring the Contours of China's Military* (Carlisle, PA: Army War College Strategic Studies Institute, 2007), 69–140.

The Annual PLA Conference

- Andrew Scobell, David Lai, and Roy Kamphausen, eds., *Chinese Lessons from Other Peoples' War* (Carlisle, PA: Army War College Strategic Studies Institute, 2011).

- Roy Kamphausen, David Lai, and Travis Tanner, eds., *Assessing the People's Liberation Army in the Hu Jintao Era* (Carlisle, PA: Army War College Strategic Studies Institute, 2014).

Every year for the last two-and-a-half decades, some of the best experts on the PLA convene for the Annual PLA Conference. Originally self-funded and held on a Virginia farm, the conference is now run by the Army War College and the National Bureau of Asian Research (NBR), who publish an edited volume of the conference papers. Like most conference and edited volumes, the Annual PLA Conference books are less coherent analyses developing particular lines of argument and more stand-alone papers linked loosely by theme or topic. No individual volume probably warrants being called indispensable, but individual chapters offer the best, most authoritative, and/or only treatment of critical issues in PLA modernization, doctrine, and military policy. These chapters provide sharp, focused, and empirically-driven assessments that, if nothing else, demonstrate the range of Chinese-language publications available to the tenacious analyst. Would-be writers could do worse than searching past volumes, which since 1999 are available for free in electronic form on the website for Army War College's Strategic Studies Institute, for relevant chapters prior to beginning their own analysis.[22]

---

[22] The Strategic Studies Institute website is now inaccessible for readers located outside the United States; however, the PDFs also are available in the digital library of The International Relations and Security Network, an online repository of analysis created by the Swiss Federal Institute of Technology Zurich <http://www.isn.ethz.ch>.

The value of these conference volumes is twofold. First, they are one of the few places to find analysis of Chinese military training exercises—a topic to which the 2012 volume and significant parts of the 2008 volume were devoted.[23] The PLA says and publishes a lot about itself, but examining Chinese training is one of the few ways to explore what the PLA does. Even if the chapters do not address training explicitly in the title, a number of the authors, who often have military experience themselves, use training and exercises to validate military writings. Second, the chapters receive a thorough review at the conference from fellow professionals who often are every bit as well-versed on the subject as the author. This review ensures that, even while the analysis remains the author's, the supporting data usually is relevant and reliable.

Although a full review of these volumes exceeds the scope of this essay, there are a handful of chapters over the years that stand out for their unique contribution to the literature of Chinese strategy and usefulness for understanding the PLA. This list cannot be comprehensive, but it should serve as a valuable introduction to the potential value lurking in the text that will not be surfaced readily through Internet searches. Furthermore, these are standard reference works within the China-watching community for their topics and are listed below in chronological order:

---

[23] Travis Tanner, Roy Kamphausen, and David Lai, eds., *Learning by Doing: The PLA Trains at Home and Abroad* (Carlisle, PA: Army War College Strategic Studies Institute, 2012); Wanda Ayuso and Lonnie Henley, "Aspiring to Jointness: PLA Training, Exercises, and Doctrine," in Roy Kamphausen, David Lai, and Travis Tanner, eds., *Assessing the People's Liberation Army in the Hu Jintao Era* (Carlisle, PA: Army War College Strategic Studies Institute, 2014), 171–206; Dennis J. Blasko, "People's Liberation Army and People's Armed Police Ground Exercises with Foreign Forces, 2002–2009," in Roy Kamphausen, David Lai, and Andrew Scobell, eds., *The PLA at Home and Abroad: Assessing the Operational Capabilities of China's Military* (Carlisle, PA: Army War College Strategic Studies Institute, 2010), 377–428; and Roy Kamphausen, Andrew Scobell, and Travis Tanner, eds., *The 'People' in the PLA: Recruitment, Training, and Education in China's Military* (Carlisle, PA: Army War College Strategic Studies Institute, 2008). One of the few examples of training exercises analyzed elsewhere is Dennis J. Blasko, Philip T. Klapakis, John F. Corbett, Jr., "Training Tomorrow's PLA: A Mixed Bag of Tricks," *The China Quarterly*, No. 146, Special Issue: China's Military in Transition (June 1996), 488–524.

- Eric Hagt, "Emerging Grand Strategy for China's Defense Industry Reform," in Roy Kamphausen, David Lai, and Andrew Scobell, eds., *The PLA at Home and Abroad: Assessing the Operational Capabilities of China's Military* (Carlisle, PA: Army War College Strategic Studies Institute, 2010), 481–551.

- Murray Scot Tanner, "How China Manages Internal Security Challenges and Its Impact on PLA Missions," in Roy Kamphausen, David Lai, and Andrew Scobell, eds., *Beyond the Strait: PLA Missions Beyond Taiwan* (Carlisle, PA: Army War College Strategic Studies Institute, 2009), 39–98.

- James Mulvenon, "PLA Computer Network Operations: Scenarios, Doctrine, Organizations, and Capability," in Roy Kamphausen, David Lai, and Andrew Scobell, eds., *Beyond the Strait: PLA Missions Beyond Taiwan* (Carlisle, PA: Army War College Strategic Studies Institute, 2009), 253–286.

- Elizabeth Hague, "PLA Career Progressions and Policies," in Roy Kamphausen, Andrew Scobell, and Travis Tanner, eds., *The 'People' in the PLA: Recruitment, Training, and Education in China's Military* (Carlisle, PA: Army War College Strategic Studies Institute, 2008), 233–289.

- David Finkelstein, "China's National Military Strategy: An Overview of the 'Military Strategic Guidelines'," in Roy Kamphausen and Andrew Scobell, eds., *Right Sizing the People's Liberation Army: Exploring the Contours of China's Military* (Carlisle, PA: Army War College Strategic Studies Institute, 2007), 69–140.

- Lonnie Henley, "War Control: Chinese Concepts of Escalation Management," in Andrew Scobell and Larry M. Wortzel, eds., *Shaping China's Security Environment: The Role of the People's Liberation Army* (Carlisle, PA: Army War College Strategic Studies Institute, 2006), 81–104.

- Kenneth W. Allen and John F. Corbett, Jr., "Predicting PLA Leader Promotions," in Andrew Scobell and Larry M. Wortzel, eds., *Civil-Military Change in China: Elites, Institutes, and Ideas after the 16th Party*

Congress (Carlisle, PA: Army War College Strategic Studies Institute, 2004), 257–277.

- Ron Christman, "How Beijing Evaluates Military Campaigns: An Initial Assessment," in Laurie Burkitt, Andrew Scobell, and Larry M. Wortzel, eds., *The Lessons of History: The Chinese People's Liberation Army at 75* (Carlisle, PA: Army War College Strategic Studies Institute, 2003), 253–292.

One of the last published volumes, *Chinese Lessons from Other Peoples' Wars*, highlights the professionalism of a military that has not been involved in major combat operations since the war with Vietnam in 1979. To compensate for this lack of experience, the PLA has devoted a great deal of intellectual effort to understanding how the United States has executed modern warfare "under high-tech conditions" as well as the wars that may reflect a cross-Strait conflict. The Chinese assessments of foreign military campaigns surveyed in this volume include the following:

- The NATO Air War in Kosovo;
- Anti-Access / Area-Denial Lessons from the Falklands War;
- Iran-Iraq Missiles Duels and Other Uses of Ballistic Missiles;
- The Gulf Wars in 1991 and 2003;
- U.S. Pacific Command Operations;
- Counterinsurgency Operations in Afghanistan (U.S.) and Chechnya (Russia).

The most important chapter in this volume is Dean Cheng's essay entitled "Chinese Lessons from the Gulf Wars," because of how much the PLA learned from how quickly the U.S. military dismantled the Iraqi military that was better equipped than the PLA at the time (pp. 153–199). The Persian Gulf War of 1990–1991 marks the entry of local wars under high-tech conditions (*gaojishu tiaojian xia jubu zhanzheng*, 高技术条件下局部战争) into the PLA lexicon, and the PLA would integrate the phrase as a key element of PLA modernization objectives in the 1993 "Military

Strategic Guidelines for the New Period" (pp. 159–160).[24] The Gulf War also impressed PLA officers with the importance of securing dominance of the electromagnetic spectrum (i.e. electronic warfare); air control as a strategic factor; operational deception; combined and joint arms operations; and the logistical support to sustain high-technology weapons (pp. 156–157). Cheng also follows these lessons through the 1990s, identifying key documents and publications where the PLA integrates the lessons from the first Gulf War into its thinking (pp. 159–163).

The second U.S. war with Iraq served to "reinforce and refine the lessons from the first Gulf War;" however, the Chinese military did draw additional lessons primarily in the realm of information operations (p. 163). PLA officers at the Academy of Military Sciences and National Defense University saw weakness across the indicators of comprehensive national power as leading to another situation where China would "suffer beatings" (*ai da*, 挨打) as Iraq did (p. 164). The PLA saw Saddam Hussein as a key part of Iraq's weakness, because of how he divided Iraq's Kurdish, Shia, and Sunni populations to the detriment of uniting the country against the United States (p. 169). Chinese analysts also addressed ostensible U.S. information operations based around the "Three Warfares" (*san zhong zhanzheng*, 三种战争, often abbreviated as *sanzhan*, 三战) concept: psychological, public opinion, and legal (pp. 170–188).[25] Although labeled

---

[24] For a discussion of these most authoritative of strategic directives, see an earlier paper delivered at the Annual PLA Conference, David Finkelstein, "China's National Military Strategy: An Overview of the 'Military Strategic Guidelines'," in Roy Kamphausen and Andrew Scobell, eds., *Right Sizing the People's Liberation Army: Exploring the Contours of China's Military* (Carlisle, PA: Army War College Strategic Studies Institute, 2007), 69–140.

[25] Dean Cheng provides detailed descriptions of the "Three Warfares," based off of translations from official Chinese sources. "Psychological warfare (*xinli zhan*, 心理战) is defined as conflict in the spiritual and psychological area and may be implemented at the tactical, operational, or strategic level" (p. 171). "Public opinion warfare (*yulun zhan*, 舆论战) refers to the use of various mass information channels, including the Internet, television, radio, newspapers, movies, and other forms of media, in accordance with an overall plan and with set objectives in mind, to transmit selected news and other materials to the intended audience" (p. 176). "Public opinion warfare is linked to the issue of values; faced with the pressure of public opinion, few nations or political authorities would risk the opprobrium associated with being an aggressor" (p. 177). Finally, "legal warfare (*falü zhan*, 法律战)is

"warfare," these concepts relate to how China sets the stage for conflict and thinks about how to position Chinese interests, so that any use of force appears justified and defensible. As such—and just like intelligence activities—they transcend war and peace. According to Cheng, the PLA came away from the Gulf Wars impressed with how the U.S. military attacked the morale of the Iraqi military through emails to unit commanders and how Washington shaped the context for both wars through the United Nations and media. While political warfare has a long history under the CCP, the Gulf Wars may have sparked a renaissance for the concept in Chinese strategic thinking and activity, as will be discussed in the subsequent section on political warfare.

The Taiwan scenario and the possibility of U.S. intervention has been one of the principle drivers of Chinese military modernization, especially after the 1995–1996 Taiwan Strait Crises[26] demonstrated the hollowness of PLA threats. The conflict most closely resembling China's Taiwan scenario is the British-Argentine war over the Falklands/Malvinas Islands in 1982, and Chinese military thinkers have produced serious, if overlooked, work on the subject (pp. 77–78).[27] Aside from obvious parallels to the Argentine position, Chinese thinkers, according to the author of this chapter, U.S. National Defense University's Christopher Yung, also have examined the British campaign for the lessons of using an expeditionary force far from home as well as how to manage political and legal issues associated with

---

defined as the use of both domestic and international law, as well as the laws of armed conflict, to garner international and domestic support by presenting oneself as the more just or virtuous side in legal terms. The basic form of legal warfare is described as arguing that one's own side obeying the law, accusing the other side of violating the law, and making arguments for one's own side in cases where there are also violations of the law" (p. 184).

[26] The 1995–1996 crises were spurred, in 1995, by Taiwan President Lee Teng-hui delivering a provocative lecture on Taiwan's place in the world independent of China and, in 1996, by Taiwan's first presidential elections. In both cases, the PLA tested ballistic missiles in the waters off of Taiwan's major ports, and the United States deployed carrier battle groups around Taiwan to deter further Chinese aggression.

[27] For another take on China's lessons from the Falklands/Malvinas War, see, Lyle Goldstein, "China's Falklands Lessons," *Survival*, Vol. 50, No. 3 (June 2008), 65–82.

[27]

territorial disputes.[28] One sign of the importance that Chinese military officers attach to this war is that the Nanjing Naval Command College dispatched research teams abroad to study the conflict (p. 79).

Chinese analysts drew both positive and negative lessons from Argentine and British conduct of the conflict across the full spectrum of military activity from the strategic setting to doctrine and operations to tactics. Foremost among the mistakes made in Buenos Aires was poor strategic assessment (in one account, "wishful thinking"), involving the underestimation of British capabilities, overestimation of Argentine capabilities, and poorly matching Argentine forces to the tasks required for defending against the British expeditionary force (pp. 81–83, 94). Of crucial importance to U.S. thinkers, Chinese analysts highlighted British logistics as both worthy of emulation and as an Achilles heel that the Argentines were too passive to exploit: "The Argentinean military philosophy was passive, its tactics inflexible … to attack Britain's most important, yet most vulnerable supply shipping; this was Argentina's greatest mistake" (pp. 83, 89–90). Closely related to logistics, Chinese thinkers saw the value of Ascension Island as a logistical hub that allowed aerial refueling to improve aerial coverage of the British task force, repacking equipment for the amphibious assault, and a safe rear area for casualty evacuation (pp. 86–87, 95, 103–104). Closing out the chapter, Yung shows how the Falklands/Malvinas lessons have become a part of PLA guidance, including the defense white papers, such as the need for expeditionary forces to carry their protection with them and to provide clear strategic guidance for military commanders (pp. 90–95).With the improvements and expansion of Chinese conventional rocket forces, including the DH-10 long-range land attack cruise missile and the DF-21D anti-ship ballistic missile, the PLA can apply some of these lessons to counter U.S. military intervention in East Asia.

---

[28] Related to the operation of an expeditionary force, see also, Andrew S. Erickson and Austin Strange, *No Substitute for Experience: Chinese Anti-Piracy Operations in the Gulf of Aden*, U.S. Naval War College, China Maritime Study No. 10 (November 2013) <https://www.usnwc.edu/Research---Gaming/China-Maritime-Studies-Institute/Publications.aspx>.

The PLA also has started analyzing counterinsurgency campaigns, indicating Beijing has concerns about its approach in Tibet and Xinjiang or, at least, thinks contingency planning should take place in case local People's Armed Police and public security elements are unable to suppress widespread unrest. In addition to analyzing U.S. operations in Afghanistan, former PLA soldier (1968–1972) and now U.S.-based academic, Yu Bin, examined how Chinese analysts from the People's Armed Police and military intelligence assessed Russian performance in the two Chechen wars. Dr. Yu's analysis is a useful example of how one can approach a small amount of data but still find constructive ways to parse it and place the arguments within the Chinese context (pp. 311–312).

In the Russian counterinsurgency experience, Chinese analysts identified a number of mistakes made by Moscow, but were complementary of Russian tactics in the Second Chechen War (1999–2009). First, Russian authorities allowed Chechen separatists time and space to organize by acquiescing to *de facto* control by the separatists (pp. 290–291). Second, Russian intelligence organizations often failed to gather accurate intelligence in contrast to their Chechen opposition, and Chinese analysts attributed at least some of the failures to organizational dysfunction and lack of coordination. Moscow, at times, seemed to have no prior knowledge of many terrorist groups, "their network, means of violence, intended targets," and financing (pp. 294, 310). Third, current Chief of Staff in the Nanjing Military Region and former chief of military intelligence Yang Hui critiqued Moscow's reliance on the military instrument—especially given the lack of preparation and training of Russian forces—at the expense of other social and economic measures to pacify the population (pp. 299–303). On the positive side of the ledger, Chinese analysts gave a positive appraisal of Russian tactics that combined the firepower of regular or special operations forces with militias with better local knowledge to hold cleared areas. A bit more controversially, Chinese analysts were divided over the use, or overuse, of Russian firepower, which was used in saturation attacks even in populated areas (pp. 303–308).

The biggest shortcoming of *Chinese Lessons from Other People's Wars* is the uneven analysis on bridging the gap between PLA lessons learned and application of those lessons. As the volume editors observe, many of the sources cited in the volume are the product of individual authors without the imprimatur of centers like those within the U.S. services for assessing and disseminating lessons learned (pp. 7–9). Political sensitivities are difficult to identify except in the most obvious cases of distortion, such as the widely divergent U.S. and Chinese analyses of the Sino-Vietnam War in 1979 or a conclusion that the Chechen insurgency could not have sustained itself "without the financial, human, and spiritual support from the West" (pp. 2, 293).[29] The two most complete analyses in this regard are Dean Cheng's aforementioned analysis and Christopher Twomey's analysis of lessons from the Iran-Iraq missile duels and other uses of ballistic missiles (pp. 115–152), where PLA materials and Chinese security policy are relatively clear.

While the proceedings of the Annual PLA Conference always offer useful information about the Chinese military, *Chinese Lessons from Other People's Wars* may be one of the most important volumes in recent years. It catalogues the PLA's vicarious experience with warfare and how it thinks China should approach the next armed conflict. This might seem a bit contradictory in light of the volume's principal fault; however, the gap between PLA analysis of lessons to be learned and the what the PLA is doing on a daily basis leaves plenty of room for analysts to contribute to the growing literature and debate about Chinese military modernization.

Hu Jintao's tenure as CCP General Secretary (2002–2012) and Central Military Commission chairman (2004–2012) witnessed dramatic improvements in PLA capabilities as the earlier reforms in the defense

---

[29] For U.S. and U.K. analysis of this conflict, see, Xiaoming Zhang, "China's 1979 War with Vietnam: A Reassessment," *China Quarterly*, No. 184 (December 2005), 851–874; Edward C. O'Dowd and John F. Corbett, Jr., "The 1979 Chinese Campaign in Vietnam: Lessons Learned," in Laurie Burkitt, Andrew Scobell, and Larry Wortzel, eds., *The Lessons of History: The Chinese People's Liberation Army at 75* (Carlisle, PA: Army War College Strategic Studies Institute, 2003), 353–378; Harlan Jencks, "China's Punitive War on Vietnam: An Assessment," *Asian Survey*, Vol. 19, No. 7 (August 1979), 801–815; Jonathan Mirsky, "China's 1979 Invasion of Vietnam: A View from the Infantry," *RUSI Journal*, Vol. 126, No. 2 (June 1981), 48–52; and James Mulvenon, "The Limits of Coercive Diplomacy: The 1979 Sino-Vietnamese Border War," *Journal of Northeast Asian Studies*, Vol. 14, No. 3 (Fall 1995), 68–88.

industries, military education, and improved budgets began bearing fruit. When the Annual PLA Conference met in 2012, the participants came together to discuss Hu Jintao's impact and the collection of papers that would become *Assessing the People's Liberation Army in the Hu Jintao Era*. Although the PLA's hardware undoubtedly improved and doctrine moved toward jointness, the two most important developments may relate to the PLA's relationship to the party and its designated role in China's development. This volume also contains several useful reference chapters on the modern context of traditional PLA concepts like "People's War" and "Active Defense" (pp. 81–128) as well as new concepts like the vague "informatization" and the PLA's approximations for the U.S. term "Anti-Access/Area-Denial" (pp. 129–170). More so than any recent PLA conference volume, *Assessing the People's Liberation Army in the Hu Jintao Era* belongs by the keyboard when writing about the PLA.

Given the importance of party-army relations, the volume appropriately opens with a chapter on the "New Historic Missions," President Hu's contribution to the party canon guiding Chinese military modernization. Shortly after Hu became CMC chairman, he gave a speech providing a new set of PLA objectives, described as the "Three Provides and One Role" (*san ge tigong, yi ge fahui*, 三个提供, 一个发挥): "provide an important guarantee for the Party to consolidate its ruling position;" "provide a powerful security guarantee for safeguarding the important Strategic Opportunity Period of national development;" "provide a powerful strategic support for safeguarding national interests;" and "to give play to the important use of safeguarding world peace and promoting common development." Although the first two missions have guided the PLA since 1949, the second two missions push the PLA to develop capabilities for operations beyond China's periphery, including, but not limited to, stability operations, anti-piracy operations, and peacekeeping operations as well as expeditionary capabilities.

CNA analyst Daniel Hartnett dissects the speech in tandem with a series of lessons for each of the "New Historic Missions" issued by the General Political Department in 2006. One of the key pieces of information contained in these sources is a clear identification of threats with the potential to derail China's development. They include the Taiwan independence movement, territorial disputes, terrorism and national separatist movements, and unidentified domestic destabilizing factors. The PLA's responsibilities for addressing these threats are self-evident, except for the need to prevent these internal threats from "joining up with 'western hostile forces'" (pp. 44–47). While a review of PLA capabilities since 2004 goes beyond the scope of Hartnett's chapter, he suggests a few areas where the "New Historic Missions" and new PLA capabilities are in congruence, most notably in the maritime, space, and cyberspace domains. Additionally, Hartnett also sees a "campaign-like attempt to reinforce [the PLA's] loyalty to the party" (pp. 35, 62–64). Because the Xi Jinping era (2012–present) has not altered the "New Historic Missions" in any significant way, this chapter remains a useful resource for understanding the PLA's role in Chinese national security. Hu's guidance also can serve as a benchmark for further analysis of PLA capabilities against the responsibilities that the party has set for the military—a point upon which the CMC agrees. In 2006, Hu's CMC issued a judgment that the PLA's current capabilities were incompatible with performing the "New Historic Missions" and with fighting and winning a local war under informatized conditions. The judgment, known as the "Two Incompatibles" (*liang ge buxiang shiying*, 两个不相适应), continues to be used through 2015 as a metric for explaining problems across all areas of PLA activities.[30]

The second contribution on the party-army relationship comes from Timothy Heath, then a senior analyst with U.S. Pacific Command and now at RAND. His chapter makes the claim that under Hu's leadership the CCP "bolstered its ability to lead a professionalizing military." His claim is threefold. President Hu tried to "strengthen the CCP as an organization, render party-military relations more functional and resilient, and improve

---

[30] Dennis J. Blasko, "The 'Two Incompatibles' and PLA Self-Assessments of Military Capability," *Jamestown Foundation China Brief*, Vol. 13, No. 10, May 9, 2013; Michael S. Chase, Jeffrey Engstrom, Tai Ming Cheung, Kristen Gunness, Scott Warren Harold, Susan Puska, and Samuel Berkowitz, *China's Incomplete Military Transformation: Assessing the Weaknesses of the People's Liberation Army (PLA)* (Washington, DC: RAND and U.S.-China Security and Economic Review Commission, 2015) <http://www.uscc.gov/Research/china%E2%80%99s-incomplete-military-transformation-assessing-weaknesses-people%E2%80%99s-liberation-army>.

the CCP's ability to provide strategic leadership" (p. 399).[31] The shift was announced in 2002 through the 16th Party Congress Work Report, which stated the CCP would become a "governing party" (*zhizhengdang*, 执政党) capable of addressing the people's fundamental interests. In the PLA context, this means improving the quality of the personnel selected as political commissars and to refocus the work of these officers toward improving the PLA's fighting effectiveness (pp. 411–412, 415–416).

Within this "governing party" paradigm, Heath also goes further than Hartnett and other analysts in underlining the importance of the "New Historic Missions."[32] For Heath, the "New Historic Missions" accomplish several things. First, they align the PLA's interests with party's interests in ways that the PLA's role in upholding CCP rule did not. Hu Jintao explicitly shifted the military's political posture into alignment to support the "governing party" paradigm and the realization of the CCP's vision for Chinese development. The PLA must "provide a stable internal and external security environment that can enable the CCP's focus on national development" (p. 419). Second, the concept is another example of how Hu began the rationalization of CCP ideology, transforming it from the inspirational to the strategic. What Heath means by the rationalization of ideology is that the CCP's Marxist-Leninist heritage now relates to a structured investigation, analysis, and creation of strategic concepts based on historical laws to guide policymaking (p. 420). If there is one shortcoming to Heath's contribution to *Assessing the People's Liberation Army in the Hu Jintao Era*, it is that his chapter is best read within the growing

---

[31] Mr. Heath explores these issues in further depth and beyond the PLA in his recent book, *China's New Governing Party Paradigm: Political Renewal and the Pursuit of National Rejuvenation* (Farnham, UK: Ashgate Publishing Co., 2014).

[32] For example, James Mulvenon, "Chairman Hu and the PLA's 'New Historic Missions'," *China Leadership Monitor*, No. 27 (Winter 2009) <http://www.hoover.org/research/chairman-hu-and-plas-new-historic-missions>. It should also be noted that, while he was an analyst at the Open Source Center, Timothy Heath was the first U.S. analyst inside or outside government to identify the "New Historic Missions" and their importance.

corpus of his work exploring the implications of the "governing party" paradigm and what it means for analyzing the CCP.[33]

Long-time PLA watcher James Mulvenon in partnership with one of his rising analysts at DGI, Joe McReynolds, fills a void in the China studies literature, both military and otherwise, in discussing the meaning of "informatization" (*xinxihua*, 信息化) in Chinese terms rather than offering vague analogies like "a Chinese revolution in military affairs." Anyone who has read more than a few pages of analysis has come across the word but left slightly puzzled by this Anglicization of the Chinese word, which Chinese writers characterize as "both a state and a process." Western analysts, as McReynolds and Mulvenon point out, have done an excellent job of cataloging the equipment, platforms, and capabilities associated with informatization, but have not explained the concept itself with any meaningful detail (pp. 208–210). Functioning as what the authors call a "concept of concepts," informatization at its most basic level "describes the process of moving toward greater collection, systematization, distribution, and utilization of information" (p. 211). The concept also operates on multiple levels, referring at times to broader, organic processes such as the "informatized conditions" for which the PLA is expected to prepare or at other times to an "intentional, directed process" such as informatization of equipment (p. 211).[34] As such, informatization in the Chinese context cannot be reduced to a military issue—even if the intrepid researcher would struggle to find anything in English about informatization in other areas—

---

[33] In addition to *China's New Governing Party Paradigm* mentioned in Footnote 7, Heath's work on this subject includes, Timothy Heath, "What Does China Want? Discerning the PRC's National Strategy," *Asian Security*, Vol. 8, No. 1 (2012), 54–72; Timothy Heath, "Why PLA Watchers Keep Missing Changes to China's Military Strategy," *American Intelligence Journal*, Vol. 27, No. 1 (Fall 2009), 67–75; and Timothy Heath, "The 18th Party Congress Work Report: Policy Blue Print for the Xi Administration," *Jamestown Foundation China Brief*, Vol. 12, No. 23, November 20, 2012.

[34] For a concise explanation of this complicated issue, Joe McReynolds also explored the informatization concept and related processes at the Third Annual Jamestown China Defense and Security Conference held in Washington, DC on February 28, 2013 in a presentation entitled "China's National 'Informatization' Effort" <http://www.jamestown.org/store/dvds>.

and the PLA also receives backing from a broader set of national policies begun in the 1990s. To explore military informatization, McReynolds and Mulvenon draw out the term's emergence in PLA publications and policy statements, making use of their knowledge of the PLA research apparatus to identify the key works, as well as the policy organizations created under Hu Jintao to coordinate informatization across the Chinese government (pp. 227–231).[35]

Informatization in the PLA has three main strands: personnel, equipment, and organization. The first goes beyond the military's recruitment, training, and promotion processes to include reforms of the PLA's research, development, and acquisition process with goal of ensuring appropriate systems for the soldiers in the force. The second covers both retrofitting and introducing new equipment to share information vertically and horizontally across the PLA's various stovepipes. The organizational component envisages a PLA with "modular" units with capabilities that can be flexibly combined to complete military operations (pp. 219–221).[36] These ideas among others surveyed by the authors illustrate that the PLA's sophistication in thinking has not been matched by the operational realities, and the organizational element is an important part of that reality (pp. 246–247). The organizational reality of the PLA, which the authors do not address in detail, includes both the dominance of the ground forces in the PLA structure and the concept of officer and unit grades (rather than rank). Officers from the ground forces dominate the General Staff Department and use the department as the army's headquarters staff, even though the PLAN, PLAAF, and Second Artillery have separate staffs for their service-specific needs.[37] Officer and unit grade determine who can give orders to

---

[35] Bates Gill and James Mulvenon, "China's Military-Related Think Tanks and Research Institutions," *The China Quarterly*, No. 171 (2002), 617–624.

[36] The "modular" groupings idea is described more fully in Kevin McCauley, "System of Systems Operational Capability: Operational Units and Elements," *Jamestown Foundation China Brief*, Vol. 13, No. 6, March 15, 2013.

[37] For a snapshot of the ground forces' dominance at the leadership transition at the 18th Party Congress in late 2012, see, Cristina Garafola, "PLA Succession: Trends and Surprises," *Jamestown Foundation China Brief*, Vol. 12, No. 24, December 14, 2012.

whom, constraining efforts to build modular forces and the PLA is still in the experimental phase of trying to reorganize the grade level to optimize coordination of combined arms operations, such as PLAN aviation flying off of an aircraft carrier (For More on Grade, see Appendix 4).[38]

These discussions of Hu Jintao's political directives and informatization are supplemented by a set of chapters that explore specific PLA developments related to these overarching themes. Defense Department analysts Wanda Ayuso and Lonnie Henley explore PLA training, exercises, and doctrinal developments from 2008 to 2012 (pp. 171–206), and former Air Force foreign area officer and assistant air attaché Kenneth Allen catalogues the PLA's international initiatives, including military-to-military diplomacy and exchanges (pp. 441–524). Two useful chapters on the PLAN's (pp. 257–300) and the Second Artillery's (pp. 301–354) capabilities were written by then-Naval War College scholars Nan Li and Michael Chase, respectively. However, neither of these capabilities chapters really brings together insights into the organizational challenges created by informatization or the PLA's doctrinal aspirations—admittedly, a difficult task.

For the generalist, these PLA Conference volumes are specialized but valuable resources that demonstrate the kind of diligent assessment throughout the hierarchy of PLA sourcing that was discussed in the "Building Blocks" section above. Since 1999, the conference volumes are free-of-charge in PDF form on the website of the Strategic Studies Institute at the Army War College. The thematic approach of each conference draws together a great deal of information about specific aspects of the PLA. The military and intelligence backgrounds of many of those involved in planning, editing, and contributing to each volume ensures that at least some analysis is forward-looking, establishing benchmarks and questions for future research. However, as some of the footnotes in this section suggest, many of the chapters that address developments in technology and equipment require an existing knowledge of the PLA and its recent past to make full use of the research and analysis contained therein.

---

[38] David Chen, "The PLA's Evolving Joint Task Force Structure: Implications for the Aircraft Carrier," *Jamestown Foundation China Brief*, Vol. 11, No. 20, October 28, 2011.

CHINESE SECURITY CONFERENCES FOR THE ADVANCED READER

- Andrew S. Erickson and Lyle J. Goldstein, eds., *Chinese Aerospace Power: Evolving Maritime Roles* (Annapolis, MD: Naval Institute Press with the China Maritime Studies Institute, 2011).
- Richard P. Hallion, Roger Cliff, and Phillip C. Saunders, eds., *The Chinese Air Force: Evolving Concepts, Roles, and Capabilities* (Washington, DC: National Defense University, Institute for National Strategic Studies, 2012) <http://www.ndu.edu/press/lib/pdf/books/chinese-air-force.pdf>.

Two books surveyed in this section come out of specialized conferences that cater to China specialists as well as military officers and government officials who deal with the implications of PLA modernization in a professional capacity. They go well beyond what is necessary for a general understanding of the PLA and its modernization drive. Unlike the Annual PLA Conference in the previous section, the focus of these conferences has not produced the same kind of conceptual knowledge about Chinese military thinking on escalation control, military-to-military diplomacy, training and education, internal security and crisis management. Nevertheless, should an analyst choose to focus on a particular service or set of capabilities, these volumes are indispensable for a deeper understanding of the Chinese military and the open sources available.

The U.S. Naval War College's China Maritime Studies Institute since 2005 has hosted an annual China Maritime Security Conference in Newport, Rhode Island. The conference papers, individually, are less substantial than either the Annual PLA Conference discussed above or the joint U.S.-Taiwan conference discussed below. Each comparatively narrowly-focused paper runs about 15 to 20 pages, but the conference volumes numerous contributions—this volume includes 27 papers—offering a level of detail on the conference theme unmatched elsewhere.[39] This volume, *Chinese Aerospace Power*, is divided into six parts with at least four contributions per section:

- Chinese Aerospace Development: Emerging Maritime Roles;
- Chinese ISR and Counter-ISR;
- Contrasting Strategies: Protecting Bastions or Projecting Power?
- Maritime Strike: Air-Launched Cruise Missiles;
- Maritime Strike: Ballistic Missiles;
- Maritime Implications of Chinese Aerospace Power.

The full scope of the book's chapters far surpasses what could be addressed in this review, but several of the chapters stand out for discussion. Two chapters on the PLA's helicopter force and airborne anti-submarine warfare (ASW) explore significant equipment deficiencies that "[defy] the conventional wisdom about the 'rapid' and 'massive' modernization of the PLA" (p. 168). These chapters demonstrate the deliberateness of PLA modernization, and the self-awareness of Chinese military thinkers about where PLA capabilities need to develop (pp. 167–169, 182–184). The issues discussed in these chapters illustrate that, despite the resources thrown at the PLA since the mid-1990s, the Chinese military still must make choices about what equipment to acquire and what programs to pursue.

One area where *Chinese Aerospace Power* makes a unique contribution is Garth Hekler's paper entitled "Chinese Early-Warning Aircraft, Electronic Warfare, and Maritime C4ISR." For Chinese linguists, Hekler outlines a basic methodology to exploit the China National Knowledge Infrastructure (CNKI) to identify influential articles in terms of readership. Among its many features, CNKI—a Chinese database that is roughly equivalent to a combination of ProQuest and JSTOR—allows researchers to organize articles by numbers of citations and views as well as by the author's affiliations to develop a proxy for influence (p. 132). Using CNKI's sorting

---

[39] For a list of the other volumes in this series, see Appendix 6.

functions, Hekler arrives at a few useful conclusions about the PLA's intent to develop electronic warfare (EW) capabilities. First, because of the physical limits on China's aircraft carrier *Liaoning*, land-based EW aircraft are an important way to improve survivability against U.S. and other advanced militaries. Second, some of the most cited articles discussed using EW to overcome electronic countermeasures to anti-ship missiles, the success of which would "improve the credibility of China's missile-based anti-access capabilities." Third, CNKI searches highlighted a Chinese focus on countering U.S.-made AGM-88 HARM "anti-radiation missiles" to maintain the integrity of China's air defense system (pp. 142–143).

Maritime legal expert Peter Dutton contributed an eerily prescient chapter about Beijing's effort to assert legal control of maritime airspace on China's periphery in light of the China's 2013 announcement of an East China Air Defense Identification Zone (ADIZ). Mr. Dutton offers one of the clearest definitions of an ADIZ available: "a zone of airspace in which a state declares that it has a security interest and for which it publishes procedures on how it expects civil aircraft to behave … to avoid the misperception that the aircraft poses a threat to the security of the state." An ADIZ has nothing to do with international borders or sovereignty (p. 91). Dutton traces the development of the international legal for maritime airspace, related to territorial rights and Exclusive Economic Zones. The most important point is that, per the Paris and Chicago Conventions, airspace is free above the seas beyond the 12-mile territorial claim (pp. 96–102). In evaluating the Chinese claim against this background, he concludes "the Chinese view is unenforceable against other states as a matter of customary international law. Customary international law is, generally, speaking, the combination of state practice and the widespread belief that the practice is required or allowed" (p. 99). The key elements here are belief and practice. If China's view is indefensible but continues to be propagated, then Dutton implies the intriguing question of whether Beijing will use its newfound power to change belief and practice along its periphery—a question some analysts have answered in the affirmative.[40]

---

[40] John Garnaut, "China's New Weapon for Expansion: Lawfare," *Sydney Morning Herald*, April 11, 2014 <http://www.smh.com.au/world/chinas-new-weapon-for-expansion-

Finally, the paper contributed by Xiaoming Zhang and Sean McClung, entitled "Challenges in Assessing China's Aerospace Capabilities and Intentions," offers a cautionary tale in critiquing other analyses of the PLA. It is hard to argue with the authors' point that inconsistencies in Western analyses "stem from source documents themselves" and, given the limited access to military publications, the *ad hoc* ways in which they were acquired and translated (p. 451). The authors also quote approvingly from an Air War College paper that cautions analysts drawing upon translations that they are "always subject to the selectivity of the passages translated, the manner of translation, and the unknown authoritativeness of many Chinese writings" (p. 451). One of the other problematic elements of Western analyses of the PLA, according to the authors, is that almost any article by a military officer or defense industry engineer can be "treated as evidence" of PLA capabilities. The authors, however, observe "As with many individual USAF publications, the purpose of these specialized periodicals is to disseminate research results, showcase theories, and stir academic debate" (p. 454).

Zhang and McClung are a little too glib about the absence of authority in PLA publications and the confusion in Western analyses. While this does not detract from the relevance of the authors' admonition, the two underestimate the effort already devoted to the question of authoritativeness. The China analysts at CNA Corporation led by David Finkelstein have developed widely-used guidance for understanding a Chinese military affairs book's authoritativeness. The volume will be published by a PLA press, on a topic well within the military's purview, for distribution throughout the PLA as teaching material as well as inputs and review from the relevant PLA departments. Moreover, authoritative books also have multiple editors, not authors.[41] Despite the authors' concern with

---

lawfare-20140411-zqtir.html>. The article also contains a link to the final version of the U.S. Department of Defense Office of Net Assessment discussed within.

[41] For an excellent example of parsing the different forms of Chinese military writing drawing upon this understanding of authoritativeness, see, Andrew S. Erickson, *Chinese Anti-Ship Ballistic Missile (ASBM) Development: Drivers, Trajectories and Strategic Implications* (Washington, DC: The Jamestown Foundation, 2013).

sourcing and confusion of aspirations with capabilities, they launch into a lengthy discussion of the PLAAF and its current state with only a few references to China's defense white papers and one of the PLA's propaganda and political warfare specialists (pp. 455–459). The irony here is China's defense white papers have a history of errata, such as adding marine brigades where none exist, and the authors make assertions, like the success of the National Defense Student Program, that fall victim to the very problems they describe.[42] And it is worth remembering that many of the PLA's aspirations of the early 2000s, such as anti-satellite weapons, electronic intelligence (ELINT) satellites, and an anti-ship ballistic missile (ASBM), did become reality less than a decade later.

Outside of any specific chapter, the book also contains a number of useful tables that catalogue important platforms and capabilities throughout the various chapters. Notable among these are Andrew Erickson's revolution and evolution table of Chinese aerospace capabilities (p. 8), Richard Fisher's catalogue of Chinese unmanned aerial vehicles (pp.124–126), Dennis Blasko's table on naval vessels capable of helicopter operations (pp. 170–172), Gabriel Collins, Michael McGauvran, and Timothy White's table on the potential gains for Chinese aircraft from aerial refueling (pp. 196–197), and Eric Hagt's appendix on China's satellite inventory and plans (pp. 396–402).

For the most part, *Chinese Aerospace Power* holds up well to developments since its publication with only one exception: the section on the Second Artillery and its ASBM, the DF-21D. The discussion about potential uses was overtaken by the deployment of China's ASBM and the publication of a comprehensive monograph on the subject.[43] Defense analyst Paul Giarra's chapter on the ASBM's implications for the U.S. Navy, however, remains a useful framework for developing an appreciation of the

---

[42] Kenneth W. Allen, "Chinese Air Force Officer Recruitment, Education, and Training," *Jamestown Foundation China Brief*, Vol. 11, No. 22, November 30, 2011.

[43] Andrew S. Erickson and Gabe Collins, "China Deploys World's First Long-Range, Land-Based 'Carrier Killer': DF-21D Anti-Ship Ballistic Missile (ASBM) Reaches 'Initial Operational Capability' (IOC)," *China SignPost*, December 26, 2010; Erickson, *Chinese Anti-Ship Ballistic Missile (ASBM) Development*.

factors Washington needs to take into account (pp. 359–374). The chapters in the final section provide an excellent overview—and guide for how to write—the implications of the Chinese military modernization efforts explored in the preceding pages.

The Taipei-based Chinese Center for Advanced Policy Studies (CAPS) is one of the few think tanks outside the United States to publish regularly on Chinese military modernization, and it has been doing so since 1992. The success of CAPS helped propel its secretary general, Andrew N.D. Yang, into Taiwan's Ministry of National Defense as deputy minister (2009–2013). Every year, CAPS hosts at least one major conference on Chinese or regional security issues with international partners—most frequently, the RAND Corporation and now often in conjunction with the U.S. National Defense University (NDU).[44] The last published volume, *The Chinese Air Force: Evolving Concepts, Roles, and Capabilities*, is the second published book coming from the renewed collaboration among CAPS, RAND, and NDU.[45]

The latest book from this PLA conference—known as the "CAPS-RAND Conference"— is the most significant book on the PLAAF since Kenneth Allen wrote the first major study of China's air force in the

---

[44] Earlier conference volumes included James Mulvenon and Andrew N.D. Yang, eds., *A Poverty of Riches: New Challenges and Opportunities in PLA Research* (Santa Monica, CA: RAND, 2004); James Mulvenon and Andrew N.D. Yang, eds., *The People's Liberation Army as Organization: Reference Volume 1.0* (Santa Monica, CA: RAND, 2002); James Mulvenon and Andrew N.D. Yang, eds., *Seeking Truth From Facts: A Retrospective on Chinese Military Studies in the Post-Mao Era* (Santa Monica, CA: RAND, 2001); and James Mulvenon and Richard H. Yang, eds., *The People's Liberation Army in the Information Age* (Santa Monica, CA: RAND, 1999).

[45] The first volume was Phillip C. Saunders, Christopher D. Yung, Michael Swaine and Andrew Nien-Dzu Yang, eds., *The Chinese Navy: Expanding Capabilities, Evolving Roles* (Washington, DC: National Defense University Press, 2011). Forthcoming edited volumes from this collaboration should include the following: "The PLA's Role in National Security Policy-Making" (2011), "Contingency Planning, PLA Style" (2012), and "The PLA 'Prepares for Military Struggle' in the Information Age: Changing Threats, Doctrine, and Combat Capabilities" (2013).

Reform Era in 1991.[46] This book combines the depth of the Annual PLA Conference papers with the breadth and focus of *Chinese Aerospace Power* in its four sections:

- Concepts;

- Organization, Leadership, and Doctrine;

- Equipment, Personnel, and Education/Training;

- Industries and Military Implications.

The first section of the book focusing on concepts of airpower begins from the broadest perspective, examining the intellectual evolution of airpower in the 20th Century from its origins emerging out of World War I to the present age of precision strike. Where previously there was substantial disagreement over the role of airpower, the proliferation of precision strike has brought agreement among most analysts that "air power is the quintessential strike element in a force-projection network able to conduct parallel attacks to create effects that are simultaneously tactical, operational, and strategic" (p. 26–27). The second chapter places airpower concepts within the China context as well as the evolution of PLAAF and Second Artillery capabilities. Although the PLAAF would want the same capabilities as their U.S. counterparts, the reality is that to date "PLA conventional air platforms have been insufficient by themselves to suppress air defenses, conduct strategic strike missions, or gain air superiority around the Chinese periphery" (pp. 33, 42–46). This has led Beijing to rely on Second Artillery for aerospace missions along with other non-traditional capabilities such as electronic warfare—a combination that gives China a potentially destabilizing advantage along its periphery, while generating regional distrust because of their asymmetry (pp. 58–59).

---

[46] Kenneth W. Allen, *People's Republic of China People's Liberation Army Air Force*, Defense Intelligence Agency, DIC-1300-445-91, May 1991 <http://www.globalsecurity.org/military/library/report/1991/plaaf-index.html>. The first study of the PLAAF was, Richard Bueschel, *Chinese Communist Air Power* (New York: Praeger, 1968), which drew the correlation between PLAAF modernization and China's economic growth and suggested air power was once considered a luxury within the PLA.

[43]

The third chapter addresses the PLA's historical, organizational, and political shortcomings that have hindered the PLAAF's development. The historical roots of the PLAAF as a defensive force—prioritizing fighters and anti-aircraft systems over bombers—reinforced by the party leadership's lack of thinking about its role in national security limited the resources directed toward the service (pp. 72–77). Organizationally, the PLAAF along with the navy and rocket forces were sidelined in leadership positons in the Military Regions and the four general departments, especially the General Staff Department, in favor of officers from the ground forces. This meant the ground forces have largely dictated the PLA's development and doctrine—a situation that only recently has begun to change with joint appointments at lower levels and more slowly at the upper echelons (pp. 81–83, 95). The personnel changes and the PLA's vigorous reform efforts following the U.S. defeat of Iraqi forces in 1991 have helped expand PLAAF influence, even if it began at a relatively low level.

The second section, particularly the first two chapters, on the PLAAF's organization constitutes the most useful element of the book for researchers. The first organizational chapter fittingly comes from Kenneth Allen who has pushed young analysts to understand organizational structure for over two decades. It provides a comprehensive overview of each of the PLAAF's departments, headquarters structure, education/training commands, and scientific research system at a minute level of detail. The knowledge gaps that Allen identifies, however, demonstrate how little is known about basic PLA decision making and responsibilities. For example, in footnote 55, he admits "no information was found that describes the specific responsibilities of the PLAAF commander, including his current role as a member of the CMC, or for the [political commissar]" (p. 127). The chapter also includes useful tables, including a comparison of U.S. Air Force and PLAAF headquarters positions (p. 100) and PLAAF officers serving in joint billets in the 2000s (p. 123). The second chapter, authored by CNA's Murray Scot Tanner, follows PLAAF discussions about its role as it undergoes a "transition from an air force focused on territorial defense toward an air force that increasingly emphasizes offensive missions and trying to seize and maintain the initiative in its combat missions" (p. 133). Tanner's survey of air force publications offers a useful summary of how the PLAAF's thinking has shifted from a defensive to an offensive mindset that sees the value of strategic strike capabilities across three mission areas: "deterring infringement of China's critical national security interests, carrying out offensive operations, and maintaining China's air and space defenses" (p. 133–134). The lightly-analytic chapter provides a lexicon for understanding how the PLAAF conceives its roles, discusses its potential, and approaches concepts like deterrence.

The second half of the book goes deeper into the broader points about PLAAF aspirations and transitions outlined above. Achieving the air force's ambitious modernization program depends on its personnel and equipment, and these chapters examine the PLAAF's ability to train its personnel and acquire or develop the equipment necessary to become a useful policy instrument. The equipment chapter, authored by RAND's David Shlapak, provides what might be the most comprehensive inventory of PLAAF aircraft, missiles, and anti-aircraft weaponry available as well as several tables comparing Chinese and U.S. equipment. Shlapak concludes "If the PLAAF is not capable of challenging U.S. airpower in a nearby scenario like a Taiwan Strait contingency, its major items of equipment are no longer the main culprits" (p. 207). The main culprits are personnel, education/training, and the sustained ability of the defense industry to outfit the air force.[47] The chapter on PLAAF education, apart from its valuable historical overview, shows the dramatic reform of this system beginning in the 1990s under President Jiang Zemin (pp. 242–251). For those with Chinese-language ability and plans to travel to Beijing, the education chapter also includes an appendix of PLAAF training publications, including both general military affairs and air force specific materials (pp. 251–252).

The PLAAF volume from the CAPS-RAND conference will be standard reference on the Chinese air force for some time to come. Despite the book's detail and comprehensiveness in drawing upon Chinese-language sources, the gaps in the knowledge about the PLAAF should encourage caution when suggesting one analyst or another is hyping or downplaying Chinese military capabilities. Some of the notable absences include the

---

[47] For one useful framework, see, Kenneth W. Allen, *The Ten Pillars of the People's Liberation Army Air Force: An Assessment*, The Jamestown Foundation, Occasional Paper (2011).

responsibilities of senior leadership and how the PLAAF evaluates the success of its educational reforms. As the Shlapak chapter implies with its judgment of the technical capacity of PLAAF capabilities, the "software" of the Chinese air force is now the most important element of understanding its capabilities in a wartime setting. Unfortunately, the PLAAF has changed dramatically since the last time it was employed against an adversary. The organizational outlines, such as provided by Mr. Allen, provide a glimpse; however, the wartime command and control of air forces in conjunction with other PLA services, because of the interlocking command relationships in PLAAF headquarters, PLA General Staff Department, and the military regions, remain uncertain as Chinese "doctrine" evolves.

These two conferences—the revitalized CAPS-RAND conference and the China Maritime Security Conference—with their push for publication have made great contributions to understanding PLA modernization in recent years. The participants fully exploit the PLA's burgeoning discussion of its requirements to meet the political leadership's demand for a military capable of "winning local wars under informatized conditions." They are illustrative of what can be accomplished with Chinese-language research in spite of the military's restrictions on what can be published in China.

The PLA's Industrial Backbone

- Tai Ming Cheung, *Fortifying China: The Struggle to Build a Modern Defense Economy* (Ithaca, NY: Cornell University Press, 2009).
- William C. Hannas, James Mulvenon, and Anna B. Puglisi, *Chinese Industrial Espionage: Technology Acquisition and Military Modernization* (New York: Routledge, 2013).
- Mikhail Barabanov, Vasiliy Kashin, and Konstantin Makienko, *Shooting Star: China's Military Machine in the 21st Century* (Minneapolis, MN: East View Press, 2012).

Looking ahead for the PLA's future potential means examining China's defense industrial base, its extant capability, and its trajectory. The three books in this section come at Chinese defense industrial modernization from different perspectives, based on the three key elements of the PLA's development: internal innovation, industrial espionage, and foreign purchasing, especially from the former Soviet states. Although China's defense industry today appears booming with two different models of stealth fighters, advanced surface warships, a panoply of short- to intermediate-range ballistic and cruise missiles, at least one aircraft carrier under construction, and an impressive suite of electronic warfare equipment, such competence is a relatively recent development. Between 1993 and 2001, China's entire defense industry ran a net loss and was "replete with examples of weapon systems with severe technological weaknesses and limitations." Only after Jiang Zemin launched a series of reforms in 1998–1999 that dramatically overhauled the defense industries, their operations, and their incentives did what we now see today become possible.[48]

---

[48] Evan Medeiros, Roger Cliff, Keith Crane, and James Mulvenon, *A New Direction for China's Defense Industry* (Santa Monica, CA: RAND, 2005), 8, 28–31.

The first book, *Fortifying China*, comes from Tai Ming Cheung, a long-time analyst of China's defense-industrial capacity who has been writing on this subject in journalistic and academic publications since the late 1980s. Cheung's experiences include being a journalist for the once-heralded *Far Eastern Economic Review*, a security and political risk analyst in Hong Kong, and, most recently, a move to academia by way of a Ph.D. from King's College London, where this book began. The book chronicles China's development of a national innovative system and modern defense industry in three periods: the Maoist era, the Reform era, and the Dual-Use era. Since the founding of the People's Republic in 1949, China's leadership has believed "an independent and vibrant defense economy as a core pillar" of the nation's pursuit of wealth and power, even when this objective has seemed like a distant goal (p. 2).

Cheung's main argument is that the Chinese defense industry has functioned best when Beijing was able to align the interests and actions of the military authorities (end users), the defense industry (producers), and civilian government authorities (regulators) (pp. 16–17). The book follows China's defense industries in both conventional and strategic arms through these three eras while exploring how end users, producers, and regulators cooperated or not. The number of factors that Cheung examines makes the book a complicated analytic narrative; however, it provides a level of detail sufficient to appreciate the nuances across China's defense economy in both the conventional and strategic weapons programs.

One of the major features of China's defense development has been the "Two Bombs, One Satellite" (*liangdan yixing*, 两弹一星) moniker, which exemplified the spirit and process of the Mao era strategic weapons programs. Even as conventional industries, like ordinance production, languished in bloated inefficiency, Beijing pushed forward with nuclear, then thermonuclear weapons, and into space at a rate belying China's technological backwardness relative to the countries achieving similar results, such as the United States, France, United Kingdom, and the Soviet Union. The model was used again in 1986 under the so-called "863 Program" (properly named the National High-Tech Development Plan) to fund "big science" projects, like advances in space, lasers, and telecommunications, rather than allowing investigator-led research to drive progress (p. 43, 238–241). The high-level leadership interest in these "big science" projects, regardless of era, provided access to resources and expertise; however, critics—notably foreign-based Chinese researchers who Beijing has tried to entice back—argued this approach was "biased, inefficient, and nontransparent and were awarded on the basis of insider connections" (p. 240). The approach here might help explain why China's defense industry has been capable of producing feats previously only accomplished by the superpowers while failing to produce more mundane and directly useful products like high-performance jet engines for modern combat aircraft.

Fortifying China is primarily about the emergence of the dual-use era in China's defense industries, and the tumultuous process that the led to where China is today. In 1978, Deng Xiaoping began the process of converting the defense industry to civilian production in line with his thinking about defense as the last of his four modernizations. These efforts included introducing contracting, allowing non-state private companies to receive contracts, and consolidating regulatory organizations into COSTIND to coordinate industry production (pp. 79–84). Initially, these measures had little effect because of a lack of consequences and the dual-hatting across end users, producers, and regulators. Changes in the 1990s, such as allowing the PLA to buy weapons from abroad, gradually placed pressure on the arms industry to reform (p. 106–108). Deng's conversion policies, however, did have the desired effect. In 1978, only 8 percent of the defense industry's output was for civilian use; in 1992, that number reached 80 percent and, in 1997, 84 percent (pp. 55, 76). The conversion process and an old policy of "combining military and civilian needs" (*junmin jiehe*, 军民结合) gradually gave way to a new directive "locating military potential within the civilian economy" (*yujun yumin*, 寓军于民), which was formally enshrined in the 2004 defense white paper (p. 184).

This final shift to a dual-use economy emerged under President Jiang Zemin, who, as a trained engineer, took a personal interest in the technical aspects of China's future security (pp. 179–180).[49] In 1998, Beijing introduced the "Four Mechanisms" (*si ge jizhi*, 四个机制) to break apart the defense industry's tenacious efforts to keep their privileged position. The "Four Mechanisms" included introducing competition, independent evaluation, external supervision to cut corruption, and encouragement for a better-motivated and -compensated workforce (pp. 130–132). In addition to allowing the PLA to contract with domestic companies, China also went abroad with "a far-reaching impact in promoting the technological development of the Chinese defense innovation system" (p. 137). Apart from the familiar purchases of whole systems and theft, China also invited hundreds of experts for consultation, bought sub-systems and components to fill specific gaps, licensed assembly in China, and pursued joint design and development (pp. 137–140). The success of these and other measures, especially related to market incentives, opened the door for innovation and the broadening of the 863 Program (pp. 183–202). The exemplars of these changes and the new defense economy come from privately-owned enterprises that developed close relationships with the PLA from the very beginning of their existence. Cheung profiles four of these companies from the telecommunications industry, namely Huawei Technologies, Great Dragon Telecommunications, Zhongxing Corporation (ZTE), and Datang Telecom Technology and Industry Group (pp. 215–222).[50]

The strength of this book is Cheung's willingness to address both the civilian and defense economies and their interrelationships—a factor that becomes increasingly important in the dual-use era. Previous treatments of this subject, such as Evan Feigenbaum's *China's Techno-Warriors*, were

---

[49] The U.S. success in the Gulf War in 1991, the Taiwan Strait crises of 1995–1996, and the U.S. bombing of China's embassy in Belgrade in 1999 alongside several high-profile instances of PLA corruption spurred Jiang to order sweeping reforms in the PLA, the selling off of PLA-owned businesses, and to fund the PLA fully in order to focus the military on protecting Chinese national security.

[50] For a thorough analysis of one of these companies, see, Nathaniel Ahrens, "China's Competitiveness: Myths, Reality, and Lessons for the United States and Japan — Case Study: Huawei," Center for Strategic and International Studies (February 2013) <http://csis.org/publication/chinas-competitiveness-huawei>.

criticized for evaluating China's defense industry with little reference to the civilian sector and hyping the role of military-industrial elite.[51] If there is any weakness, it is the overwhelming number of acronyms that are required to simplify writing about the alphabet soup of the Chinese organizational landscape. In conjunction with a relatively poor index, *Fortifying China* does not serve easily as a reference and can be skimmed only with difficulty. Cheung writes a detailed narrative about a complicated subject that does require nuance. Beijing's ability to drive missile and nuclear programs effectively has not translated evenly over the conventional sector, where, even today, China's progress is uneven. And, because the narrative is primarily focused on China's organizational landscape and national innovation system, Cheung only touches upon China's acquisition and integration of foreign technology (pp. 137–142).

Since at least the 1980s, China has become one of the most significant international actors in the theft of U.S. and other Western military-related technologies.[52] Although Beijing denies such accusations as products of Cold War thinking, U.S. judicial proceedings, congressional investigations, and Chinese sources have provided an overwhelming body of evidence that licit and illicit foreign technology acquisition has fueled the rapid pace of Chinese military modernization. The first book to pull this all together in a coherent picture is *Chinese Industrial Espionage: Technology Acquisition and Military Modernization* written by veteran PLA watcher James Mulvenon and two U.S. Government analysts without a prominent public presence.[53] This book goes well beyond previous treatments, such as the congressional inquiry led by Christopher Cox in the late 1990s, by providing a

---

[51] Richard P. Suttmeier, "China's Techno-Warriors: Another View," *The China Quarterly*, No. 174 (September 2004), 804–810.

[52] William Overend, "China Seen Using Close U.S. Ties for Espionage: California Activity Includes Theft of Technology and Surpasses That of Soviets, Experts Believe," *Los Angeles Times*, November 20, 1988 <http://articles.latimes.com/1988-11-20/news/mn-463_1_chinese-espionage>.

[53] This section is adapted from Peter Mattis, "A Professional Assessment of Chinese Espionage," *International Journal of Intelligence and Counterintelligence*, Vol. 28, No. 2 (March 2015).

comprehensive assessment of how China acquires foreign technology and integrates it into existing programs.

The most important contributions of this volume center on the dismissal of the notion of amateurish Chinese collection and the firm differentiation between the activities of China's intelligence services and its technology collectors. Hannas, Mulvenon, and Puglisi make a strong case against the conventional perspective on Chinese intelligence operations that treats all collection activity as having the same character, whether the target is intellectual property, technological widgets, or national security information. These analysts demonstrate different *professional* systems function in parallel, but not necessarily in coordination, to collect foreign science and technology.

In the United States, we tend to think of the clandestine intelligence disciplines—for example, human intelligence, signals intelligence, and geospatial intelligence—requiring professional expertise, while downplaying the professional requirements of open source intelligence (OSINT). Based on the account in *Chinese Industrial Espionage*, China however has treated OSINT in science and technology with the same professionalism that the United States has adopted for the clandestine arts. The authors state "Whereas all science begins with prior art, in China the systematic use of foreign sources to promote [science and technology] development has been elevated literally to an 'information/intelligence science' (*qingbaoxue*, 情报学)" (p. 18). The second chapter traces the origin of that science and the organizations that practice it—a development institutionalized in 1956. The State Council described the goal of this system as the following:

> "The responsibility of [science and technology] intelligence work is to report the most recent accomplishments and trends in domestic and foreign science ... [necessary] to facilitate the absorption of modern scientific and technological accomplishments, reduce time and manpower, avoid duplication of work, and promote the development of science and technology in China" (p.19).

Over time, this OSINT collection system would develop all the identifiable hallmarks of professionalism, including professional associations, specialized training and education, and a corporate body of knowledge in a professional literature. The chronicling of China's system for exploiting open sources probably is the most important chapter in the book, because of the challenge it puts in front of the conventional view that Chinese intelligence collection is a process driven by amateurs (pp. 18–51). These Chinese collectors may be amateur clandestine operators; however, they are professional collectors and indexers of useful scientific and technological information for the purposes boosting China's industry.

The second valuable contribution of *Chinese Industrial Espionage* is the cataloguing of the various Chinese policies and organizations that promote technology transfer to China. In three chapters—"Trade for Technology" (pp. 52–77); "PRC-Based Technology Transfer Organizations" (pp. 78–104); and "U.S.-Based Technology Transfer Organizations" (pp. 105–135)—the authors provide a convincing catalogue of organizations that deserve more scrutiny for understanding their role in technology transfer, both licit and illicit. These chapters may be somewhat lacking in analysis; however, the authors still provide enough direct quotes and documentation of the links between the Chinese government and ostensibly non-governmental associations to raise red flags. The book also covers China's students abroad, traditional espionage operations run by the intelligence services, and computer network exploitation with reasonable and persuasive detail.

In many ways, this book shows the hidden side of China's military modernization, which has gone from backward and lagging behind Iraq in 1991 to one of the world's foremost militaries with niche capabilities that are world class.[54] The authors judge "While giving due credit to the Chinese people for their ability to produce, China could not have engineered this transformation, nor sustained its progress today, without cheap and unrestricted access to other countries' technology" (p. 2). They also cite estimates from knowledgeable Chinese sources that publicly note their systematic acquisition of foreign technological information reduced research costs by 40–50 percent and time by 60–70 percent (p. 38). One can

---

[54] For a brief discussion, see, Robert Farley, "What Scares China's Military: The 1991 Gulf War," *The National Interest*, November 24, 2014 <http://nationalinterest.org/feature/what-scares-chinas-military-the-1991-gulf-war-11724>.

only wonder how those figures have changed today with China's cyber exploitation of foreign companies to bolster the open source collection.

Although readers may find it difficult to wade through the dense, heavily-sourced writing, even experienced China experts and intelligence junkies will find new information. The sourcing from Chinese government websites, journal articles, and newspapers supplements the more accessible U.S. documentation. The transparency applied by the authors makes this book a lasting and useful reference guide that demonstrates how much information is truly available for the diligent researcher. For the analyst without Chinese-language skills, this book should replace nearly all previous discussions about Chinese industrial espionage and, to a lesser extent, the activities of the Chinese intelligence services.[55]

The final volume in this section, *Shooting Star*, is a translation from a Russian report produced by the Moscow-based Centre for Analysis of Strategies and Technologies (CAST). Given how important Soviet- and Russian-built equipment has been for the PLA modernization process, the Russian perspective based on Chinese- and Russian-language research is one that should not be overlooked.[56] In addition to substantial reports like *Shooting Star*, CAST also produces shorter reports on a variety of issues including Chinese industrial espionage and defense industries. To access CAST publications in English, the reader will need to go through East View Information Services, which is also responsible for making databases like the China National Knowledge Infrastructure available in the United States.

The report is organized into three chapters: China's Defense Industry, China on the Arms Market, and Chinese Arms Exports. The first chapter

---

[55] For example, David Wise, *Tiger Trap: America's Secret Spy War with China* (New York: Houghton Mifflin Harcourt Publishing Company, 2011); Howard DeVore, *China's Intelligence and Internal Security Forces* (Coulsdon, UK: Jane's Information Group, 1999); and "Special Report: Espionage with Chinese Characteristics," StratFor, March 24, 2010.

[56] After a down period beginning in 2007, Beijing has or is attempting to purchase newer Russian equipment, including the S-400 long-range surface-to-air missile and the Su-35 fighter—both of which fill distinct PLA needs. See, Wendell Minnick, "S-400 Strengthens China's Hand in the Skies," *Defense News*, April 18, 2015; Zachary Keck, "Problem: China Still Wants Russia's Deadly Su-35 Fighter," *The National Interest*, May 4, 2015.

offers a brief overview of China's key defense contractors, their various corporate subsidiaries, and two case studies on the Chinese shipbuilding and aircraft engine industries. The second chapter addresses China's position in the international arms market, especially its cooperation with and purchases from Russia after the post-Tiananmen U.S. and European arms embargo. According to the report, Chinese contracts accounted for 40 to 45 percent of all Russian arms exports, peaking at 60 percent in 2000 (p. 51); however, since 2007, China's importance for Russia has fallen dramatically. The chapter also provides a comprehensive list of Russian systems sold to or jointly produced with the Chinese (pp. 52–62). The final chapter explores what armaments China produces for international sale, who buys them, and future trajectories for Chinese weapons exports.

The analytic portions of *Shooting Star*, unfortunately, are too short and far between, but the busy reader will find the authors' judgments accessible and straightforward. For example, in the shipbuilding case study, the authors highlight the PLA Navy's expertise and hardware for air defense, anti-submarine warfare, and anti-mining operations as significant vulnerabilities and connect these shortcomings to potential international arms suppliers (pp. 22, 35). While these naval problems are not exactly unknown,[57] the book's value here and elsewhere comes from the connections drawn to potential arms suppliers and the references to the Russian, Ukrainian, and Belarussian defense industries.

The most valuable elements of *Shooting Star* are the country-by-country, weapon-by-weapon accounts of Chinese arms exports, technical cooperation, and PLA inventory. Where appropriate the authors identify the related Russian systems or critical components. This makes the book a good starting point when searching for Chinese weapon systems, their background, and their availability on the international market. This is not a book that will earn any literary awards; however, the discussion of individual weapons systems explains some of the deficiencies in PLA combined arms operations. For example, under the heading "Airborne and Anti-Ship Missiles," the authors explain "China did not have any tactical

---

[57] For example, Lyle Goldstein, "China Confronts a Long-Standing Weakness in Anti-Submarine Warfare," *Jamestown Foundation China Brief*, Vol. 11, No. 14, July 29, 2011.

air-to-surface missiles in its arsenal until it secured deliveries from Russia in the late 1990s" (p. 118).

For those tracking the Chinese conventional arsenal, *Shooting Star* offers a somewhat-dated (circa late 2011) inventory of the PLA. Nevertheless, the extensive tables and references will ease the work of building up one's own database. The excellent index also adds to the book's value as a reference work.

Between *Fortifying China*, *Chinese Industrial Espionage*, and *Shooting Star*, the reader will develop a comprehensive and detailed perspective on the infrastructure associated with China's military modernization. Although other noteworthy books have been published and Cheung continues to lead a research project at UC San Diego that produces edited conference volumes, these three books will form the foundation for years to come.[58] They accurately capture the defense industry reforms of the 1980s and 1990s as well as the bottlenecks, such as aircraft engines, that continue to plague the Chinese armaments industry. Any forward-assessment of Chinese defense modernization should consider these aspects of a military's development, and these researchers have shown that Chinese sources provide an ever-widening picture of how even a topic as sensitive as the defense industry can be made accessible.

---

[58] For example, Tai Ming Cheung, ed., *Forging China's Military Might: A New Framework for Assessing Innovation* (Baltimore, MD: Johns Hopkins University Press, 2014).

Propaganda and Political Warfare

- Larry M. Wortzel, *The Dragon Extends Its Reach: Chinese Military Power Goes Global* (Herndon, VA: Potomac Books Inc., 2013).

- Andrew Chubb, "Propaganda, Not Policy: Explaining the PLA's 'Hawkish Faction' (Part One)," *Jamestown Foundation China Brief*, Vol. 13, No. 15 (July 2013); "Propaganda as Policy? Explaining the PLA's 'Hawkish Faction' (Part Two)," *Jamestown Foundation China Brief*, Vol. 13, No. 16 (August 2013).

- Mark Stokes and Russell Hsiao, *The People's Liberation Army General Political Department: Political Warfare with Chinese Characteristics*, Project 2049 Institute, Occasional Paper (October 2013).

One of the realities of analyzing China is that Beijing actively attempts to distort foreign and even domestic understanding of its politics, intentions, and capabilities. Despite widespread knowledge of this fact, analysts only recently have tried to come to grips with the purpose and implications of the cacophony of Chinese voices on foreign affairs and national security. The aforementioned hierarchy of sources serves as a good rule of thumb for separating the wheat from the chaff in the Chinese media; however, reliance on the hierarchy precludes interrogation of these other voices. In a tightly-regulated media environment, it makes little sense to avoid an important set of regularly-heard voices. In this sense, the impetus created by uninformed generalists citing fiery PLA-affiliated commentators in the commercial media has forced the China-watching community to address questions filtered out by the focus on authoritative voices.

In a wide-reaching survey of how the PLA is adapting to the global set of demands that China's leadership has placed upon it, former army attaché Larry Wortzel offers one of the few general PLA analyses to integrate Chinese political and information warfare into its narrative. *The Dragon Extends Its Reach* does provide a thorough introduction to some of the basic features of the PLA, its history and its structure in addition to a quick survey of modernization in the ground forces, navy, air force, and strategic rocket forces. The primary argument of the book is that the PLA is extending its global reach because of two key drivers: the PLA needs to counter U.S. superiority in each of the warfare domains and the need to develop capabilities to protect China's expanding interests abroad.

Unlike some of the more thorough treatments noted above, these individual chapters offer effective snapshots that capture key issues that most likely will interest the generalist—specialists are more likely to find corresponding chapters in *Strategic Asia 2012–13: China's Military Challenge* volume useful. Of particular note are Wortzel's chapters on Chinese C4ISR (pp. 27–44), space warfare and space control (pp. 117–132), and information warfare and the Chinese concept of "Integrated Network Electronic Warfare" (*wangdian yitizhan*, 网电一体战) (pp. 133–150). The chapters are too short to give a complete accounting of Chinese capabilities, doctrine, and implications; however, they do capture PLA modernization in an accessible way across a broad swath of recent technical developments. The unique contribution of Wortzel's work, however, is the discussion of China's effort to shape foreign perceptions in a chapter entitled "The General Political Department and Information Operations" (pp. 151–162).

Here, Wortzel introduces the aforementioned PLA information operations concept called the "Three Warfares", comprised of "Media Warfare" or "Public Opinion Warfare" (*yulun zhan*, 舆论战); "Psychological Warfare" (*xinli zhan*, 心理战); and "Legal Warfare" (*falü zhan*, 法律战). In a largely descriptive analysis, Wortzel fleshes out the PLA's role in China's wide-ranging perception management efforts. The first, "Public Opinion Warfare," deals primarily with efforts to frame national security-related issues in a light favorable to China. The targets include domestic and foreign audiences to persuade both of "the rectitude of China's policies and actions" and reinforce the legitimacy of the CCP's rule (p. 152–154). The second, "Psychological Warfare," is targeted at adversaries and potential adversaries to undermine the "will to fight and is designed to lower the efficiency of enemy forces by creating dissent, disaffection, and dissatisfaction" (pp. 154). The third, "Legal Warfare," focuses on using domestic and international law to garner support at home and abroad for the use of force, ranging from the kind of low-level coercive action seen in the South and East China Seas up to and including war.

One of the weaknesses of Wortzel's treatment of the "Three Warfares" is that many of the examples he uses do not involve the Chinese military—a fault that he acknowledges (p. 153). For example, he highlights the global spread of China's Confucius Institutes as an example of China's political warfare, because of the potential to exploit language learning to influence thinking about China as well as the party. The military role within the Confucius Institute program is negligible to nonexistent, and Wortzel does nothing to show such connections. Despite this weakness of not focusing on what the PLA does specifically within the "Three Warfares" framework, Wortzel highlights that perception management and influence operations are a whole-of-government operation for the People's Republic and the CCP. Party elements, such as the United Front Work Department, and state-controlled elements, such as China Central Television (CCTV), play a significant role in promoting China's image and interests.

Remarkably, one of the best contributions to understanding the non-authoritative PLA voices comes from an Australian Ph.D. student, Andrew Chubb, whose focus is on the intersection of Chinese propaganda, public opinion, and foreign policy. In a two-part series for the Jamestown Foundation's *China Brief*, Chubb profiles some of the most vocal PLA-affiliated foreign affairs commentators—including Luo Yuan, Dai Xu, and Zhang Zhaozhong—and explores how they may reinforce Beijing's domestic and foreign agenda. Instead of dismissing their incendiary rhetoric—like suggesting that China turn the Diaoyu/Senkaku Islands into a military target range—or presuming them to be manifestations of China's political factions, Chubb builds a case that these men are part of, rather than users of, the Chinese propaganda system.[59]

---

[59] For an alternative argument, see, Yawei Liu and Justine Zheng Ren, "An Emerging Consensus on the U.S. Threat: The United States According to PLA Officers," *Journal of Contemporary China*, Vol. 23, No. 86 (2014), 255–274. For Chubb's discussion and measured response, see, "Are China's Hawks Actually the PLA Elite After All?" *South Sea Conversations*, December 5, 2013 <https://southseaconversations.wordpress.com/2013/12/05/are-chinas-hawks-actually-the-pla-elite-after-all>.

The strongest pieces of evidence supporting his assessment are the description that many of these Chinese pundits used to describe their work. For example, Luo Yuan said his role as a "rational hawk" must be "designed properly at the highest level," and he has described himself as doing "military external propaganda work." Answering questions about the discrepancy between seemingly outrageous statements and his more professional analysis, Zhang Zhaozhong responded that being a CCTV commentator required "first of all, attention to politics, discipline, and the overall situation," because CCTV is "the party's propaganda and public opinion front line." Finally, Chubb quotes Dai Xu offered the following remarks at the PLAAF Political Academy:

> "In all these years in so many different places, being involved in many secret work units, writing a lot of internal reports, providing a lot of internal reference material to the highest leaders, on one hand doing internal work, on the other doing external work, I have always firmly grasped the two strands: there is nothing off-limits in thinking, but propaganda is subject to discipline."

In addition to these comments, Chubb examines how the commentators respond to and follow military regulations about public commentary, blogs, and Weibo (China's Twitter). The "hawks" are not out-of-control commentators; however, their role as propagandists does not mean that their statements should be taken word-for-word. If the goal is to shape the domestic and international environment, then emotional and psychological effect is more important than the specific words.

In the second part, Chubb explores the question of what value Beijing gets from having such hawkish—and sometimes even critical—voices in the public discourse. Externally, their provocative statements seem to make Beijing's positions and intentions seem more moderate, encouraging compromise rather than risk inflaming popular Chinese sentiment as Japan and the Philippines in tacitly accepting a new status quo during recent tensions. Domestically, they promote what is called "imperilment consciousness," the sense that foreign powers threaten to derail China's rise to prominence. While many have suggested party's promotion of nationalism is a double-edged sword, Chubb's research indicates that, contrary to the assertions of Chinese interlocutors, Beijing may actually want the hawkish public opinion. In essence, the "hawks" enable rather than constrain Chinese policymaking, and Chubb has since gathered survey data that undermines the notion that nationalism constrains Chinese foreign policymaking and the ability to compromise on maritime disputes.[60]

The shaping of Chinese public opinion to enable policy and to promote deterrence would certainly qualify as part of the "Three Warfares." What is lacking from Chubb and Wortzel's analysis is sustained and coherent examination of the PLA organizations involved. This oversight is what creates the aforementioned holes in Wortzel's analysis. Anyone looking at the PLA for any length of time will come across the "four general departments" (*si zongbu*, 四总部). They will be hard-pressed, however, to find much on the General Political Department (GPD) apart from its role as the party's political watchdog inside the military. Known primarily for his work on China's conventional and nuclear missile programs, former U.S. Air Force foreign area officer Mark Stokes with Russell Hsiao at the Project 2049 Institute have opened up a new line of inquiry into the understanding the understudied GPD. The General Political Department performs a number of functions within the PLA, including approving promotions, managing the political commissars who function as unit co-commanders, and, of course, political warfare.[61]

Political warfare, according to the report, is synonymous with "liaison work" (*lianluo gongzuo*, 联络工作), managed appropriately by the GPD's Liaison Department.[62] The department's mission can be described as "active measures to promote the rise of China within a new international

---

[60] Andrew Chubb, *Exploring China's "Maritime Consciousness": Public Opinion on the South and East China Sea Disputes*, Perth USAsia Centre, November 26, 2014 <http://perthusasia.edu.au/publications/Maritime-Consciousness-Attitudes-Report>.

[61] The best description available of the GPD can be found here, Larry Wortzel, "The General Political Department and the Evolution of the Political Commissar System," in Mulvenon and Yang, eds., *The PLA as Organization 1.0*, 225–246.

[62] In the U.S. and U.K. governments, the Liaison Department is most often known as the Liaison Office of the General Political Department (LO/GPD or GPD/LO).

order and defend against perceived threats to state security," especially in the political and psychological domains. Today, this operates at the "nexus of politics, finance, military operations, and intelligence" at least in part because of the close connections between the Liaison Department and the scion's of China's elite families known as "princelings" (p.3). In contemporary American terms, the Liaison Department's work could best be characterized as a variation of public diplomacy; however, this Americanism does not include the idea "winning without fighting," Sun Tzu's acme of skill that finds modern articulation in works like *The Science of Military Strategy*. Public diplomacy also is communicated through public channels where the standing and intent of the speaker is clear. The Liaison Department's activities obscure who is speaking for what purpose.

Liaison work, according to the *Chinese People's Liberation Army Political Work Regulations* reissued in 2003 and cited by Stokes, serves three purposes in addition to its focus on Taiwan: "conduct enemy disintegration [and] rallying friendly military work"; "investigate and research the situation of foreign militaries, enemy militaries, and national separatists inside and outside [China]"; and "guide [Chinese] force's conduct of psychological warfare research and training." These regulations also provided the first formulation of the "Three Warfares" discussed above. Underpinning these efforts is "investigation and research" (*diaocha yanjiu*, 调查研究), which, beyond general social and political research on a target country, includes compiling dossiers of individual policymakers and social figures to facilitate influencing them (p. 15).

By piecing together a wide variety of sources, Stokes and Hsiao also provide a historical account of the Liaison Department's activities as well as an organizational overview. Many of the sources relate to the career paths of individuals. Tracking officials also allows an interesting insight into Beijing's handling of Taiwan policy. During the 1980s, Liaison Department officials, rather than foreign affairs specialists or other security officials, dominated the Taiwan Affairs Leading Small Group, Beijing's foremost policymaking body for Taiwan-related issues (pp. 12–13). Tracking personnel appointments through event summaries, company and government websites, as well as comparing overlapping contact information allows a dogged researcher to piece together Chinese organizations that would otherwise be invisible from public view. This approach is not perfect as Stokes' many caveats make clear, but the Liaison Department and its public activities are now more visible. Tracking individuals also reveals the overlapping connections between Chinese corporations and liaison work, revealing that Liaison Department officials appear to be mid-level officers, never junior, who often have a variety of experience outside the PLA (pp. 22–31). Unfortunately, this approach only allows the researcher to sketch the contours of China's liaison work rather than come to any decisive conclusion about the effectiveness and coordination of the different bureaucratic elements.

The research into the PLA's propaganda system for national security purposes is still in its early phases;[63] however, the results are a testament to what can come from diligent research in Chinese-language sources. The generalist and the non-linguist may not ever be able to duplicate this kind of research, but they should be aware of it. That such research can be conducted seems to indicate that the Chinese consider their language to be the basic level of encryption and that Chinese security officials face similar challenges as their Western counterparts in trying to contain the flow of potentially sensitive information out into the open world.

---

[63] Analysis of the propaganda system and its role in reinforcing the CCP's domestic rule is much better developed. See, for example, Anne-Marie Brady, *Marketing Dictatorship: Propaganda and Thought Work in Contemporary China* (Lanham, MD: Rowman and Littlefield, 2007); Anne-Marie Brady and Wang Juntao, "China's Strengthened New Order and the Role of Propaganda," *Journal of Contemporary China*, Vol. Vol. 18, No. 62 (2009), 767–788; and David Shambaugh, "China's Propaganda System: Institutions, Processes, and Efficacy," *The China Journal*, No. 57 (January 2007), 25–58.

STRATEGIC ASIA AND THE CHINA CHALLENGE

- Ashley J. Tellis and Travis Tanner, *Strategic Asia 2012–13: China's Military Challenge* (Seattle, WA: The National Bureau of Asian Research, 2012).

- Ashley J. Tellis, Abraham M. Denmark and Travis Tanner, eds., *Strategic Asia 2013–14: Asia in the Second Nuclear Age* (Seattle, WA: The National Bureau of Asian Research, 2013).

For the last 14 years, the National Bureau of Asian Research (NBR) based in Seattle, Washington, has published an edited volume, *Strategic Asia*, which provides a country-by-country, regional, and thematic review of key issues in the Asia-Pacific region. Although China has a chapter each year with a rotating authorship that is a who's who list of experts on Chinese foreign policy—past authors include Thomas Christensen, Kenneth Lieberthal, and David Shambaugh—NBR decided to devote an entire volume to the impact of Chinese military modernization three years ago. The second-to-last volume covered the nuclear weapons posture and ambitions across East Asia with a China chapter written by Jeffrey Lewis, Director of the East Asia Non-Proliferation Program at the Monterrey Institute of International Studies.

The *Strategic Asia 2012–2013* volume provides a set of chapters from a collection of the best analysts of the PLA and of regional security. Though the title *China's Military Challenge* indicates a clear focus on China's military modernization program and its regional implications, this volume continues the past practice of adopting country studies. Authored by Dan Blumenthal (United States), Christopher Hughes (Northeast Asia), Arun Sahgal (India), and Andrew Shearer (Southeast Asia and Australia), these chapters examined the responses to Chinese military modernization undertaken in their respective country or region but go beyond the scope here. The PLA-focused chapters offer tightly written studies of the evolution in China's force posture in the following areas: ground forces, PLAAF and PLAN aviation, C4ISR and "informatization," and conventional missile forces.

The first substantive chapter focuses on the development of the PLA's ground forces from the Deng Xiaoping era forward. Authored by former U.S. Army foreign area officer Roy Kamphausen, who served in Beijing as an assistant army attaché in the 1990s and in the Office of the Secretary of Defense, the chapter is an exemplar of how to write an effective analysis of the PLA without invoking reams of Chinese-language sources. Mr. Kamphausen is able to do this, because his sources are selective but sound. First, Mr. Kamphausen draws on the English-language translations of China's defense white papers and English-language Xinhua reports on uncontroversial military developments. Second, among Western sources, he primarily uses Dennis Blasko's aforementioned *The Chinese Army Today* and chapters from the annual PLA Conference, now convened by NBR and the Army War College, to structure his use of other, more current sourcing.

For the PLA ground forces, according to Kamphausen, the 1990s saw a dramatic change in China's security environment and Beijing's concern with future power projection needs. These combined to diminish the ground forces relative importance among the PLA services. The expansion of the People's Armed Police to take over internal security missions and the disappearance of the Soviet threat along the northern border substantially reduced the need for massive ground forces (pp. 30–35). Kamphausen argues the very different security situations now faced on China's different borders have diversified the ground forces' roles—adding, for example, counterterrorism and cooperative security with the former Soviet republics (pp. 46–51).

The prolific Andrew Erickson contributed the chapter on PLA aviation, adopting a clean framework for appreciating the strategic impact of Chinese airpower. The chapter begins with discussion of Chinese national interests, based on the Chinese concepts underpinning PLA modernization, such as the "main strategic direction" and the "New Historic Missions" (pp. 63–67). Following a brief description of China's capabilities, Erickson judges "achievements remain uneven, and actual combat capabilities are uncertain."

[65]

Looking ahead, he offers an informed set of judgments about the likely progress of Chinese power projection, which is broken down carefully in a series of tables providing thumbnail sketches of Beijing's emergent blue water capabilities (pp. 84–85, 88). Erickson is careful to parse his assessments of Chinese capabilities to specific areas, and this lends credence to his claim that the PLA will develop strong capabilities in China's near seas, but "farther afield, Beijing will probably continue to rely on the global system, from which it benefits as a free or minimum-payment rider" (p. 94).

Erickson's nearly 30-page appendix cataloguing systems across the PLAAF and PLAN is an invaluable bookmark for the Chinese military's inventory of naval vessels, fixed- and rotary-wing aircraft as well as UAVs (pp. 99–125). The tables also flush out Erickson's sketches of Chinese aviation and naval capabilities. For the analyst working up their own Chinese order of battle charts, Erickson provides a short one-page explanation of how the tables were constructed using a variety of sources from the Pentagon's annual reports, *Jane's Defense Review*, and *The Military Balance* published annually by the Institute for International and Strategic Studies to Google Earth imagery of PLAN and PLAAF bases (p. 98).

The PLAAF largely developed as a defensive force controlling most of China's fighter aircraft and anti-aircraft artillery, offering Beijing with few options for ground support and conventional, long-distance strike. The Second Artillery, China's strategic missile force, has taken up this role with a growing arsenal of conventional missiles, ranging from short- to intermediate-range ballistic missiles to the DF-21D anti-ship ballistic missile to the long-range DH-10 land-attack cruise missile (pp. 129–130). Former U.S. Air Force assistant air attaché Mark Stokes tackles the Second Artillery in his contribution to *China's Military Challenge*, and he brings considerable time on target to the evaluating the present and future capabilities of the Second Artillery. This time on target shines through in his organizational breakdown of the missile forces, which includes identification of the missile bases, their armaments, their organizational structure, and their identification numbers known as Military Unit Cover Designators (MUCD) (pp. 131–140).

In the absence of PLA capabilities to assert air and sea control, Stokes makes a convincing case that the Second Artillery is central to Chinese deterrence and counter-intervention (*fanganshe*, 反干涉, known in U.S. parlance as anti-access/area-denial [A2/AD]).[64] One of the ways in which to see this importance is the PLA investment in the Second Artillery's C4ISR infrastructure, which in addition to access national-level, space-based intelligence assets includes a burgeoning unmanned-aerial vehicle (UAV) program (pp. 147–149). Given the importance of these missiles to Chinese military power and widespread access to *The Science of Second Artillery Campaigns*, one might wish that Stokes had examined how the Second Artillery intends to use their missiles against potential adversaries more closely. Luckily, other sources—lacking Stokes' attention to organizational detail—do provide those answers.[65]

Kevin Pollpeter's chapter on China's space, cyber, and electronic warfare capabilities adopts a different tack, eschewing organizational analysis and providing an organized description of key Chinese writings on these capabilities. Unfortunately, by asking one, albeit impressive, analyst to address these disparate capabilities[66] in one chapter, the editors prevented the kind of analysis that brought interests, capabilities, and trajectories into a coherent framework with the organizational outlines of they are

---

[64] For an important discussion of counter-intervention, see, Christopher P. Twomey and M. Taylor Fravel, "Projecting Strategy: The Myth of Chinese Counter-Intervention," *The Washington Quarterly*, Vol. 37, No. 4 (Winter 2015), 171–187.

[65] For example, Michael S. Chase and Andrew S. Erickson, "The Conventional Missile Capabilities of China's Second Artillery Force: Cornerstone of Deterrence and Warfighting," *Asian Security*, Vol. 8, No. 2 (2012), 115–137, and Ron Christman, "Conventional Missions for China's Second Artillery Corps: Doctrine, Training, and Escalation Control Issues" in Andrew S. Erickson and Lyle J. Goldstein, eds., *Chinese Aerospace Power: Evolving Maritime Roles* (Annapolis, MD: Naval Institute Press with the China Maritime Studies Institute, 2011), 307–327.

[66] Chinese space capabilities include intelligence and communications as well as ground-based anti-satellite weapons. Cyber includes electronic warfare as well as strategic and operational intelligence. And electronic warfare, apart from cyber, includes a variety of ground-based and airborne jammers.

employed.[67] The author, nevertheless, provides a quick introduction to Chinese thinking on how to apply these capabilities within the PLA and against adversaries for command and control, intelligence collection, and electronic warfare. And *Strategic Asia* is at least a cheaper alternative to other works on Chinese information operations.[68]

Strategic Asia 2012–2013: China's Military Challenge continues the series' adept approach at understanding the Asian strategic environment. Thanks in part to what is probably the strongest editorial process at any U.S. think tank, the PLA chapters offer excellent templates for writing on the PLA that is intended for a general audience. Each chapter follows a similar logic beginning from interests and stated intentions to capabilities—both actual and intended—to the future impact of China's military modernization. Each chapter functions as a self-contained report, because the analytic framework explicitly exists within the chapter and the authors address both concepts and actual capabilities. The addition of order of battle tables in each PLA-focused chapter adds greatly to the value of this volume for someone learning about the Chinese military, because the tables here go into detail on the PLAN, PLAAF, and Second Artillery complementing Blasko's detail in *The Chinese Army Today* on the ground forces.

Jeffrey Lewis' chapter in the most recent *Strategic Asia* volume may be the best single paper on Chinese nuclear posture and strategy available. Lewis moves rapidly and with authority through China's development of nuclear weapons through current controversies over China's stockpile and commitment to a "No First Use" policy to implications for the United States. For an analyst known for his caustic wit and sarcasm, Lewis surprisingly begins his discussion of the policy implications with a sensible caution:

---

[67] For a sense of the complexity of the organizational landscape, see, Mark Stokes and Ian Easton, *China's Electronic Intelligence (ELINT) Satellite Developments: Implications for U.S. Air and Naval Operations*, Project 2049 Institute (February 2011), esp. 4–5.

[68] For example, Timothy L. Thomas, *Decoding The Virtual Dragon - Critical Evolutions In The Science And Philosophy Of China's Information Operations And Military Strategy - The Art Of War And IW* (Ft. Leavenworth, KS: U.S. Foreign Military Studies Office, 2007).

"Modesty should therefore be the catchword of all analyses of China's nuclear force posture and strategy: the outside world cannot fully know the country's strategic capabilities, understand how its leaders think about nuclear weapons, or predict how those leaders may leverage nuclear weapons in a crisis or conflict" (p. 92).

Analytic modesty and Lewis' concern about China's "surprising" nuclear developments, however, do not open the door to speculation based on unreliable sources. And controversy over China's nuclear weapons illustrates some of the pitfalls of research today on China. Beginning in 2008, former Pentagon official and adjunct Georgetown professor Phillip Karber with a group of his students conducted a wide-ranging research project into China's tunnel complexes. Written up in the *Washington Post*, the project generated controversy from its conclusion that China's 3,000-mile long network of tunnels might be hiding up to 3,000 nuclear warheads—an order of magnitude higher than the 80 to 400 warheads most official reports and most experts, including Lewis, think China possesses.[69] Although the main focus of the study was the tunnel network, Karber drew on several unverified and, in some cases, discredited sources that claimed to be based on Chinese military documents to speculate about the size of China's nuclear arsenal.[70] Lewis does not rehash his online analysis—which highlights the need to estimate nuclear arsenals based on the available fissile materials and to be careful of press claims about numbers and capabilities on technical military issues—but goes carefully through the argument for a Chinese arsenal of several hundred warheads.

---

[69] William Wan, "Georgetown Students Shed Light on China's Tunnel System for Nuclear Weapons," *Washington Post*, November 29, 2011
<http://www.washingtonpost.com/world/national-security/georgetown-students-shed-light-on-chinas-tunnel-system-for-nuclear-weapons/2011/11/16/gIQA6AmKAO_story.html>.

[70] Jeffrey Lewis, "Collected Thoughts on Phil Karber," *Arms Control Wonk*, December 7, 2011 <http://lewis.armscontrolwonk.com/archive/4799/collected-thoughts-on-phil-karber>; Gregory Kulacki, "The Sources of Karber's Sources," *All Things Nuclear*, Union of Concerned Scientists, December 7, 2011 <http://allthingsnuclear.org/the-sources-of-karbers-sources>.

Lewis' argument is threefold. First, the availability of plutonium and several assessments, including a leaked Department of Energy report, place the upward boundary of China's arsenal around 700 warheads. Second, China's nuclear development and strategy has been premised on the "minimum means of reprisal," requiring only a survivable arsenal that can enough damage to give an opponent pause. Mao's view of the atom bomb as a "paper tiger" was rooted in the belief that conflict was decided by men and politics, not material factors. There is no indication that Chinese leaders or military strategists have revisited, much less revised, these assumptions about war (pp. 80–82). Third, the logic of nuclear deterrence suggests China hiding the size of its arsenal does make sense. Lewis writes "Although there is some deterrence benefit for China to uncertainty about the size of its nuclear forces, that benefit exists only for smaller arsenal sizes. There would be little advantage in concealing an investment in a deterrent that is underestimated by such a large margin" (p.79).

Since China first tested an atomic bomb in 1964, Beijing has maintained a "No First Use" policy on nuclear weapons. Whether Chinese leaders actually would follow this policy in a war with Russia, the United States, or any other nuclear power has been debated hotly. Despite being known for his sarcastic criticisms, Lewis coolly addresses the recent question of whether China revisited its policy on "No First Use." In 2013, China's biannual defense white paper *The Diversified Employment of China's Armed Forces* omitted its usual language reiterating the policy, prompting speculation that Beijing was changing its policy.[71] The small size of China's arsenal and military writings about nuclear strategy has encouraged disbelief about whether Beijing means what it says, but Lewis writes "much of what has been viewed as a debate about [No First Use] is actually a debate about generating realistic options within that framework" (p. 79).

In addition to his clear-headed assessment of China's approach to nuclear weapons, Lewis also provides a useful reminder that China's strategic environment is more complicated than the United States, Japan,

---

[71] James Acton, "Is China Changing Its Position on Nuclear Weapons," *New York Times*, April 19, 2013 <http://www.nytimes.com/2013/04/19/opinion/is-china-changing-its-position-on-nuclear-weapons.html>.

and Taiwan. For example, while relations with Russia have improved since the end of the Cold War, many of Beijing's nuclear decisions, such as launching the DF-31 intercontinental ballistic missile program in 1985 (fielded in 2008), were made when rivalry rather than cooperation characterized Sino-Russian relations (p. 88). Moreover, there is the complicated Chinese relationship with India, involving territorial disputes, and the close partnership with Pakistan, including Beijing's long support of that country's nuclear program. The latter also complicated relations with United States, because of how Chinese equipment and technical documents ended up circulating internationally through the A.Q. Khan network (pp. 90–91).

The one limitation of Lewis' chapter is that it is an assessment of the current state of play, of current external knowledge on Chinese nuclear posture. Most beneficially, however, Lewis himself recognizes the need for modesty about future developments, noting "Time and again, outside observers of China's nuclear policy and strategy have been surprised by the scope of its nuclear capabilities and the speed of its modernization" (p. 92). Lewis is far from the only observer to suggest the speed or pathway of PLA modernization has diverged from analysts' estimates, and this problem in PLA watching is one of which every would-be analyst should be aware.[72]

---

[72] In 2009, former U.S. Pacific Commander Admiral Robert F. Willard told reporters in Seoul that he "would contend that in the past decade or so, China has exceeded most of our intelligence estimates of their military capability and capacity every year. They've grown at an unprecedented rate in those capabilities," see, Bill Gertz, "Inside the Ring: China Estimate War," *Washington Times*, November 5, 2009; John Pomfret, "Defense Secretary Gates: U.S. Underestimated Parts of China's Military Modernization," *Washington Post*, January 9, 2011 <http://www.washingtonpost.com/wp-dyn/content/article/2011/01/09/AR2011010901068.html>; David Shambaugh, "China's Military Modernization: Making Steady and Surprising Progress," in Ashley Tellis and Michael Wills, eds., *Strategic Asia 2005–06: Military Modernization in an Era of Uncertainty* (Seattle, WA: The National Bureau of Asian Research, 2005).

Conclusion and Takeaways

The wealth of information now available on the PLA is both a blessing and a curse for the generalist seeking to develop their thoughts on China. The PLA watchers have exploited the continuing boom of Chinese sources on the PLA, leading to more and more specialized literature.[73] Ten years ago, a leading China scholar presciently suggested David Shambaugh's *Modernizing China's Military* (2003) might be the last book published that provides comprehensive coverage of the PLA with any authority, given the commercialization of PLA presses and the explosion of information on the Internet, including PLA newspapers.[74] Every subsequent attempt to cover the full scope of PLA capabilities and trajectories has had to make substantial choices about what to cover. This requires would-be writers on China to cast a wider net for sourcing than they would hope to understand Chinese national security and military affairs. There is no one-stop shop for understanding today's PLA. Navigating the literature is not an easy task for those who are just starting out and trying to read in to the subject.

The books and edited volumes surveyed above offer a few generalizations about where readers should seek the best work on the PLA. First, former military officers, especially those with military attaché and foreign area officer experience, are the foundation of the community. This experience is shared among many of the names that keep cropping up: Dennis Blasko, Bud Cole, Mark Stokes, David Finkelstein, Kenneth Allen, John Corbett, Susan Puska, Edward O'Dowd, and more. These individuals

---

[73] James Mulvenon and Andrew N.D. Yang, eds., *A Poverty of Riches: New Challenges and Opportunities in PLA Research* (Santa Monica, CA: RAND, 2004) <http://www.rand.org/pubs/conf_proceedings/CF189.html>.

[74] James Mulvenon, "Review of David Shambaugh, *Modernizing China's Military: Progress, Problems, and Prospects* (Berkeley, CA: University of California Press, 2003)," *The China Quarterly*, No. 177 (March 2004), 215–216.

have built up extensive databases in their areas of interest, combining the experience, time on target, and repeated efforts to explain a complex and evolving organization in familiar terminology. Second, the U.S. military service colleges, federally-funded research and development centers (FFRDCs), and defense contractors are now the primary producers of publicly-available analysis of the PLA. This is not happening at traditional think tanks and universities. With a few notable exceptions, most rising specialists who are getting published work in one of these three places. Third, there are very few "current" or even "periodic" publications that the generalist can turn to for reliable and regular analysis. Only by focusing on individuals and organizations can the generalist acquire a satisfying selection of research materials and exemplars for how to research the PLA.

This review essay aimed to provide a bridge and a roadmap for those trying to develop their expertise on the PLA and begin contributing to the ongoing discussion about China. No amount of discouragement can overcome the demand for more analysis of China or the need for individuals to write their way through their thoughts about how to deal with China. It is not unreasonable, however, to expect a higher standard of research, thinking, and writing. The stakes are too high for a few salty quotes from Sun Tzu to qualify as expertise. In an age when each piece of news may be re-blogged and recycled repeatedly, getting it right the first time is more important than ever.

Even equipped with the knowledge and roadmap above, the generalist or student, who wants to become an effective contributor to the discussion of the Chinese military challenge, faces a daunting task. The humbling reality is that very little original research on the PLA can be done anymore without Chinese language skills, especially with the cutoff of public access on December 31, 2013 to the English translations produced by the U.S. Open Source Center (previously the Foreign Broadcast Information Service, FBIS). Without these reports once available through the World News Connection, English-language resources now are limited to Western news reports and official Chinese media to supplement secondary sources.

Just developing China expertise and reading into the PLA, however, cannot be enough. As Rudyard Kipling once wrote of such parochialism, "And what should they know of England who only England know?"

CONCLUSION

Reading beyond the PLA about military and strategic affairs more generally is an underestimated element of developing expertise on China's military. All militaries have shared functional requirements from personnel management to logistics to combat. War is one of the oldest human activities, and people have been writing about it since history started being recorded. Especially in the area of military affairs, as British strategist Basil Liddell Hart wrote, "There is no excuse for any literate person to be less than three-thousand years old in his mind." Useful starting points abound in professional reading lists and the bibliographies in more recent works on strategy, but a few personal favorites can be found in this footnote.[75] Additionally, a short reading list related to analyzing foreign militaries is provided in Appendix 3.

Below are a few of the consistent features of the best analysis of the PLA and, more generally, Chinese security issues.

- *Transparency*: The best analysis of the PLA consistently identifies the logic underpinning its analysis, explaining what sources are chosen, the framework used, and walking the reader through the steps. Reasonable people disagree about China's policy and military capabilities—even the existence of a Chinese strategy. Although largely descriptive work can sometimes be exempt from this, any

---

[75] The Strategic Studies Core Reading list of Johns Hopkins University School of Advanced in International Studies drawn up by Eliot Cohen is one useful starting point for developing this broader base of expertise <https://www.sais-jhu.edu/sites/default/files/core_readings_current.pdf>. Another exemplary reading list is the Australian "Chief of Army's Reading List," which includes annotated bibliographic entries and an essay by Lieutenant General Paul van Riper (USMC, Ret.) on professional military education <http://www.army.gov.au/Our-future/Publications/Chief-of-Army-Reading-List>. The U.S. Naval Institute website hosts links to all of the U.S. military reading lists <http://www.usni.org/naval-institute-press/reading-lists>. An old syllabus from the National War College also provides a provide overview of national security decision making and the political-military linkages that make strategy effective <http://www.resdal.org/Archivo/d00000a0.htm>. In addition to these reading lists, the following article serves as a good starting point for basic questions about how well a military performs: Allan R. Millett, Williamson Murray, and Kenneth H. Watman, "The Effectiveness of Military Organizations," *International Security*, Vol. 11, No. 1 (Summer 1986), 37–71.

discussion of strategy, intentions, and future capabilities almost requires the author elaborate on the choices he/she is making.

- *Aim for Authority*: The Chinese system has a relatively clear hierarchy of authority in its publications. With the PLA's vast educational and research establishment, many conflicting ideas float side-by-side with statements of policy. The former obviously should be treated with caution, while the latter should be scrutinized. Moreover, the propaganda system for shaping internal and external views complicates any analysis that is not done without attention to sources and sourcing. Choosing sources with care and purpose ensures quality, and, at times, the reader will welcome additional information describing why a particular source was used.

- *Chinese Sourcing*: The growing availability of Chinese-language sources on the PLA now outstrips the translation resources available. Chinese-language skills are now a requirement to developing into a serious analyst. Alternatives, however, are there for the intrepid analyst. First, Chinese military thinkers do draw extensively from Western strategists, including the classic works from Carl von Clausewitz and Alfred Thayer Mahan.[76] Grounding in these classics, as long as they are used prudently, can offer another way to analyze the PLA while keeping within the parameters of Chinese debate and concepts. Second, in addition to Xinhua and Chinese Military Online (http://eng.chinamil.com.cn) for news items, key Chinese works, like *The Science of Military Strategy*, are now available in English.

- *Keeping an Open Mind*: China's military modernization consistently has surprised observers, and even some of those most forward-looking assessments of the PLA underestimated how far and how fast it actually developed.[77] For example, China analysts once pilloried

---

[76] James Holmes and Toshi Yoshihara, *Chinese Naval Strategy in the 21st Century: The Turn to Mahan* (New York: Routledge, 2008).

[77] For an overzealous but still useful analysis of this issue, see, Amy Chang with John Dotson, *Indigenous Weapons Development in China's Military Modernization*, U.S.-China Security and Economic Review Commission, April 5, 2012.

[75]

CONCLUSION

Richard Fisher in the 1990s for alleging that China planned on building an anti-ship ballistic missile, but, as of 2012, the PLA has deployed the DF-21D with a terminal guidance system that may allow it to strike ships at sea.[78] The PLA is not like the U.S. military (nor other Western militaries), and both have different industrial bases, professional competencies, and ways of thinking about war. An open mind, however, does not give license to fantasy but rather to appreciation that the PLA might develop different solutions to old military problems because of its history, how it identifies and defines challenges, and available resources.

- *Searching for Topics*: Finding interesting topics can be a challenging exercise; however, the PLA and the Chinese leadership often identify areas of importance. On important dates (e.g. New Year's and Army Day) and important national meetings (e.g. party plenums and National People's Congress sessions), the major media outlets often carry thematic editorial series and articles/speeches by senior military officials that address issues of concern to military decision makers. In addition to the thematic concerns, key phrases also can appear that describe official judgments about military modernization, capabilities, and direction. Analytic discoveries, like Hu Jintao's "New Historic Missions," came from just such searching of high-profile editorials, speeches, and party documents.

- *Defense White Papers as Starting Points*: When considering a topic and thinking about how to research it, one of the best places to begin is the biannual defense white paper. Available in both Chinese and English, they offer statements on a wide range of military policy issues and PLA priorities. Not every topic will be addressed in successive iterations of the defense white paper, so it can be

---

<http://www.uscc.gov/Research/indigenous-weapons-development-china%E2%80%99s-military-modernization>.

[78] Richard D. Fisher, Jr. "China's Missile Threat," *Wall Street Journal*, December 30, 1996; Erickson, *Chinese Anti-Ship Ballistic Missile (ASBM) Development:*.

CONCLUSION

worthwhile to go back further if the most recent white paper has not discussed the researcher's interest.

- *Organizational Recordkeeping.* For all of Beijing's shiny new military equipment to be useful, it still must fit into the PLA's organizational structure. Knowing how the PLA fits together, or at least the part of it that one is evaluating, helps strengthen analysis by addressing the basic questions of "who?" and "where?" which in turn helps answer the "why?" and "how?" The works surveyed above, especially *The Chinese Army Today*, *PLA as Organization v2.0*, and *Strategic Asia 2012–2013*, offer a starting point from which to begin more current analysis. One of the best tools is keeping track of Military Unit Cover Designators (MUCD or, in Chinese, 部队). Many Chinese news reports only identify the MUCD, a general location, or a base, so identifying and connecting these data points opens up a great deal more information to the researcher than would be available through direct searches.

The following appendixes provide additional materials and a select bibliography on the PLA and Chinese security affairs. In conjunction with the sources analyzed above, they should provide a clear roadmap for finding relevant sourcing and analysis on the PLA and several other topics related to Chinese security.

APPENDIXES

1.	Sources for China-Related Analysis	79
2.	Understanding China	83
3.	Analyzing Foreign Militaries	85
4.	Key Concepts and Phrases	86
5.	The PLA Watchers	92
6.	Select PLA and Chinese Security Bibliography	96
7.	The 1990s Revolution in the PLA	118
8.	The PLA and the Party	119
9.	Chinese Government Documents	120
10.	Core Chinese-Language Readings	123
11.	Works Reviewed (In Order)	126

APPENDIX 1: SOURCES FOR CHINA-RELATED ANALYSIS

In addition to tracking individual analysts (Appendix 5) and their organizations, there are a few regular publications and online resources of which everyone should be aware. The resources highlighted below focus primarily on using Chinese sources to analyze China; thus, they make a lot of material available for non-linguists to digest. Once again, these are only starting points and introductions to the larger discussions taking place.

- The Jamestown Foundation *China Brief* is a biweekly electronic journal that publishes four articles and the editor's column on Chinese political, military, foreign policy, and economic affairs. The *China Brief* operates in the niche between academic analysis published with a six- to 18-month time lag and the daily media cycle. The articles, generally, are based on Chinese sources in addition to other sources local to the question, so may include Indian, Japanese, Philippine, and other sourcing. <http://www.jamestown.org/programs/chinabrief>

- Published under the aegis of the Hoover Institution at Stanford, the *China Leadership Monitor* is a quarterly electronic journal. Edited by Alice L. Miller, a veteran China analyst with past experience as an open source analyst for the U.S. Government, the journal engages some of the best and most experienced analysts of China in the United States. Each issue includes thematic analysis, including foreign policy, national security, and the PLA. <http://www.hoover.org/publications/china-leadership-monitor>

- The Institute for National Strategic Studies at the U.S. National Defense University now has a Center for Chinese Military Studies. Directed by Phillip Saunders, the Center publishes the *China Strategic Perspectives* occasional paper series. Although the output is irregular, the quality of the papers and the writers are high.

- The China Maritime Studies Institute at the U.S. Naval War College publishes a robust occasional papers series *China Maritime Studies*. Topically, the reports range from civil-military relations to maritime law and Chinese naval capabilities with an eye toward how the issue impacts China's navy and U.S.-China interactions. These reports often include multiple authors and resemble short books rather than essays or a typical think tank report. <http://www.usnwc.edu/Publications/Publications.aspx>

- The Institute on Global Cooperation and Conflict at UC San Diego publishes issue briefs related to its project on the Study of Innovation and Technology in China (SITC). These are short versions of conference papers, which are slowly being compiled and published in edited volumes such as *Forging China's Military Might*. The SITC project began in 2009, funded primarily from the U.S. Department of Defense's Minerva Initiative. In addition to their conferences, SITC also runs a summer workshop on the relationship between security and technology in China. <http://www-igcc.ucsd.edu/research/technology-and-security/innovation-and-technology-in-china/sitc-publications/sitc-policy-briefs86327.php>

- The *China Vitae* leadership database is a useful starting point for finding information about China's civilian and military leadership. The database primarily provides translations of Xinhua's Chinese-language leadership pages as well as other official catalogues of leaders' activities, speeches, and travels. <http://www.chinavitae.com>

- The Tokyo-based National Institute of Defense Studies (NIDS), a Japanese think tank connected to the Ministry of National Defense, produces a *Chinese Security Report* and an annual *East Asian Strategic Review* as well as irregular policy briefs. Although written in Japanese, NIDS also provides high-quality English translations of their publications and occasionally Chinese versions. <http://www.nids.go.jp/english>

- The Project 2049 Institute in Arlington, VA produces several reports each year on Chinese military-related matters, based on careful Chinese-language research. The think tank has tackled a range of subjects—apart from the political warfare study reviewed above—addressed nowhere else, including nuclear warhead handling and

SOURCES FOR CHINA-RELATED ANALYSIS

China's signals intelligence service, in addition to their expertise on Chinese aerospace. <http://www.project2049.net>

- The congressional U.S. China Economic and Security Review Commission (USCC) publishes an annual report every November that, in part, surveys Chinese security developments of the last year. The USCC also issues shorter topical reports and commissions testimony worthy of attention. <http://www.uscc.gov>

- The National Defense Authorization Act (2000) required the U.S. Department of Defense to produce an annual report on Chinese military power, entitled the *Military and Security Developments Involving the People's Republic of China*. <http://www.defense.gov/pubs>

- *Andrew Erickson's Personal Website* offers regular updates and links to newly-released documents, statements, and studies related to the PLA. Dr. Erickson is one of the most prolific writers on the PLA today, and his writings can be found at the aforementioned places as well as *China SignPost* and the *Wall Street Journal*'s China Real Time report. <http://www.andrewerickson.com>

- *Popular Science*'s *Eastern Arsenal* Blog, authored by Jeffrey Lin and Director of Brooking's Center for 21st Century Security, provides several posts each month primarily on Chinese military hardware developments drawing from Chinese online forums and news. <http://www.popsci.com/blog-network/eastern-arsenal>

- Bill Bishop's *Sinocism Newsletter* offers regular updates of what's happening in China, providing a roundup of recently-published news and analysis. Mr. Bishop, a Beijing-based former journalist and entrepreneur, is a voracious reader and he highlights readings in both Chinese and English often on a near daily basis. <https://sinocism.com>

- Founded by Dr. Philip Yang in 1997, *Taiwan Security Research* sends out a weekly newsletter aggregating news and analysis related to Taiwan's security and regional security in East Asia. The website archives past articles going back several years organized by record type (e.g. news,

APPENDIX 1

comments, polls, and speeches) and by topic (e.g. Taiwan, U.S.-China relations, and cross-Strait). <http://www.taiwansecurity.org>

- The Congressional China Caucus distributes a daily email newsletter with a few links to mostly security-related China news stories and analysis. Register to receive the *Caucus Brief* through the China Caucus website, and past issues are available here. <http://forbes.house.gov/chinacaucus/blog>

- Taiwan's Ministry of National Defense publishes a variety of reports in Chinese and English related to the PLA and its defense, such as the *ROC Quadrennial Defense Review* and the *National Defense Report*. The National Security Bureau director also gives annual testimony to the Legislative Yuan on Taiwan's threat environment and political-military developments across the Taiwan Strait.

- A handful of well-known analysts post regularly on Twitter, mostly in the form of links to articles on daily news related to Chinese foreign policy and security matters. Most notable are the aforementioned Bill Bishop (@niubi), M. Taylor Fravel (@fravel), Andrew S. Erickson (@AndrewSErickson), and Andrew Chubb (@zhubochubo). Follow them for useful links to breaking news and analysis.

- Non-Chinese speakers obviously cannot draw from the *PLA Daily* (解放军报) or other military speeches and writings in CCP journals, like *Seeking Truth* (求是), to say nothing of the specialized or professional literature. They do, however, have recourse to the *PLA Daily* English-Language Web Portal, which contains a substantial, albeit filtered, amount of information on exercises, senior officer appearances, military-to-military contacts, and major events like the National People's Congress. <http://english.chinamil.com.cn>

- The Chinese Ministry of National Defense also provides leadership pages for the Central Military Commission members. Each CMC member's page contains English-language news articles on their activities, appearances, and meetings with foreign leaders. <http://eng.mod.gov.cn/Database/Leadership/index.htm>

APPENDIX 2: UNDERSTANDING CHINA

In this author's experience, some analyses of Chinese security neglect the broader domestic and international context in which Beijing makes decisions. This list, where appropriate, includes both an academic reference and a non-fiction alternative for easier consumption. These books provide a crash course in understanding China today beyond its military dimensions.

China's Political System

- Kenneth Lieberthal, *Governing China: From Revolution to Reform*, 2nd Edition (New York: W.W. Norton & Company, 2003).

    Alternative: Richard McGregor, *The Party: The Secret World of China's Communist Rulers* (New York: HarperCollins Publishers, 2010).

- Timothy Heath, *China's New Governing Party Paradigm: Political Renewal and the Pursuit of National Rejuvenation* (Farnham, UK: Ashgate Publishing Co., 2014).

- Susan V. Lawrence and Michael F. Martin, *Understanding China's Political System*, R41007, March 20, 2013 <http://fas.org/sgp/crs/row/R41007.pdf>.

- June Teufel Dreyer, *China's Political System: Modernization and Tradition*, 9th Edition (Upper Saddle River, NJ: Pearson Education Inc., 2014).

U.S.-China Relations

- Robert Suettinger, *Beyond Tiananmen: The Politics of U.S.-China Relations, 1989–2000* (Washington, DC: The Brookings Institute Press, 2003).

- Warren Cohen, *America's Response to China: A History of Sino-American Relations* (New York: Columbia University Press, 2010).

    Alternative: James Mann, *About Face: A History of America's Curious Relationship with China, From Nixon to Clinton* (New York: Alfred A. Knopf, 1998).

China Today and Tomorrow

- Jonathan Fenby, *Will China Dominate the 21st Century* (Cambridge, UK: Polity Press, 2014).

- Daniel Lynch, *China Future's: PRC Elites Debate Economics, Politics, and Foreign Policy* (Stanford, CA: Stanford University Press, 2015).

- Damien Ma and William Adams, *In Line Behind a Billion People: How Scarcity Will Define China's Ascent in the Next Decade* (Upper Saddle River, NJ: Pearson FT Press, 2013).

- Jeffrey Wasserstrom, *China in the 21st Century: What Everyone Needs to Know*, 2nd Edition (New York: Oxford University Press, 2013).

    Alternative: Evan Osnos, *Age of Ambition: Chasing Fortune, Truth, and Faith in the New China* (New York: Farrar, Straus, and Giroux, 2014).

    Alternative: Philip P. Pan, *Out of Mao's Shadow: The Struggle for the Soul of a New China* (New York: Simon & Schuster, 2008).

APPENDIX 3: ANALYZING FOREIGN MILITARIES

In a mirror image of the previous appendix, some China analysts neglect a functional understanding of security. In their training, they do not necessarily receive a good introduction to security, strategy, and military affairs as well as organizational matters. The selections in this appendix were chosen for their relevance to analyzing foreign militaries.

- Michael Herman, *Intelligence Power in Peace and War* (Cambridge: Cambridge University Press, 1996).
- Beatrice Heuser, *The Evolution of Strategy: Thinking War from Antiquity to Present* (Cambridge: Cambridge University Press, 2010).
- Edward Luttwak, *Strategy: The Logic of War and Peace*, Revised Edition (Cambridge, MA: The Belknap Press, 2002).
- Thomas Mahnken, *Uncovering Ways of War: U.S. Intelligence and Foreign Military Innovation, 1918–1941* (Ithaca, NY: Cornell University Press, 2009).
- Ernest R. May, ed., *Knowing One's Enemies: Intelligence Assessment Before the Two World Wars* (Princeton, NJ: Princeton University Press, 1984).
- Allan R. Millett and Williamson Murray, eds., *Military Effectiveness: The First World War; The Interwar Period; The Second World War*, 2nd Edition [3 Volumes] (Cambridge: Cambridge University Press, 2010).
- Jörg Muth, *Command Culture: Officer Education in the U.S. Army and the German Armed Forces, 1901–1940, and the Consequences for World War II* (Denton, TX: University of North Texas Press, 2012).
- Patrick Porter, *Military Orientalism: Eastern War through Western Eyes* (New York: Columbia University Press, 2009).
- James Q. Wilson, *Bureaucracy: What Government Agencies Do and Why They Do It* (New York: Basic Books, 1989).
- Arnold Wolfers, *Discord and Collaboration: Essays on International Politics* (Baltimore, MD: Johns Hopkins University Press, 1965).

APPENDIX 4: KEY CONCEPTS AND PHRASES

This appendix provides quick references and descriptions of important Chinese phrases and PLA concepts. Below each description are bibliographic references to analysis and further elaboration for each entry.

"New Historic Missions" **(新的历史使命):** On December 24, 2004, incoming Central Military Commission Chairman Hu Jintao promulgated the "New Historic Missions" for the PLA. The "New Historic Missions" provided four missions: (1) consolidate the Chinese Communist Party's ruling status; (2) ensure China's sovereignty, territorial integrity, and domestic security to continue national development; (3) safeguard China's expanding national interests; and (4) help maintain world peace. The "New Historic Missions" provide the guiding framework for PLA missions beyond territorial defense and reunification with Taiwan.

- Daniel Hartnett, "The 'New Historic Missions': Reflections on Hu Jintao's Military Legacy," in Roy Kamphausen, David Lai, and Travis Tanner, eds., *Assessing the People's Liberation Army in the Hu Jintao Era* (Carlisle, PA: Army War College Strategic Studies Institute, 2014), 31–80
<http://www.strategicstudiesinstitute.army.mil/pubs/display.cfm?pubID=1201>.

- 胡锦涛 [Hu Jintao], "认清新世纪新阶段我军历史使命 [See Clearly Our Military's Historic Missions in the New Century of the New Period]," December 24, 2004 <http://gfjy.jxnews.com.cn/system/2010/04/16/011353408.shtml>.

"Active Defense" **(积极防御):** China's Ministry of National Defense describes "Active Defense" as the PLA's strategic concept that "adheres to the principle of featuring defensive operations, self-defense and striking and getting the better of the enemy only after the enemy has started an attack." This concept has caused some confusion among some Western analysts, who have seen Beijing as willing to launch offensive campaigns like the tactical surprises of the Sino-Indian War (1962) and the Sino-Vietnamese War (1979). The central point of confusion is at what point Chinese leaders believe "an attack" has started and, therefore, believe China should respond with force. This is a strategic judgment that Chinese strategists do not think precludes tactical surprise and initiative: "Striking only after enemy has struck does not mean waiting for the enemy's strike passively ... for the 'first shot' on the plane of politics must be differentiated from the 'first shot' on that of tactics" (*The Science of Military Strategy*).

- Paul H.B. Godwin and Alice L. Miller, *China's Forbearance Has Limits: Chinese Threat and Retaliation Signaling and Its Implications for a Sino-American Military Confrontation*, China Strategic Perspectives No. 6 (Washington, DC: National Defense University Institute for National Strategic Studies, 2013).
- Peng Guangqian and Yao Youzhi, eds., *The Science of Military Strategy* (Beijing: Military Science Publishing House, 2005). This is the English-language translation of the 2001 edition.

"Two Incompatibles" (两个不相适应): The "Two Incompatibles" are a judgment about PLA capabilities established by the Central Military Commission and Hu Jintao in a *PLA Daily* editorial published on January 1, 2006. The "Two Incompatibles," according to the editorial, was defined as the following:

> "The main contradiction in our army building is that the level of our modernization is incompatible with the demands of winning a local war under informatized conditions, and our military capabilities are incompatible with the demands of carrying out the army's historic missions in the new century and new stage."

The "Two Incompatibles" judgment has since been joined and amplified by the phrases "Two Large Gaps" (*liang ge chaju hen da*, 两个差距很大), "Two Inabilities" (*liang ge nengli bugou*, 两个能力不够), and "Three Can or Cannots" (*san ge nengbuneng*, 三个能不能).

- Dennis J. Blasko, "The 'Two Incompatibles' and PLA Self-Assessments of Military Capability," *Jamestown Foundation China Brief*, Vol. 13, No. 10, May 9, 2013.
- Michael S. Chase, Jeffrey Engstrom, Tai Ming Cheung, Kristen Gunness, Scott Warren Harold, Susan Puska, and Samuel Berkowitz, *China's Incomplete Military Transformation: Assessing the Weaknesses of the People's Liberation Army (PLA)* (Washington, DC: RAND and U.S.-China Security and Economic Review Commission, 2015) <http://www.uscc.gov/Research/china%E2%80%99s-incomplete-military-transformation-assessing-weaknesses-people%E2%80%99s-liberation-army>.

"Military-Civil Integration" (军民融合): Sometimes translated as "Civil-Military Integration" (and, in Chinese, *junmin yitihua*, 军民一体化), "Military-Civil Integration" has four components in Chinese policy. The first and most well-known component relates to the integration of the defense industry with the civilian economy. The second is national defense education, which, as defined by the 2004 Defense White Paper, serves "to enhance the national defense awareness of the people" and provide "education in patriotism." The third is joint military and civilian efforts to secure PLA facilities and communications. The final component is national defense mobilization for military use of civilian resources in wartime. It also includes integrating demobilized soldiers into civilian government posts as a way to improve coordination.

- Daniel Alderman, Lisa Crawford, Brian Lafferty, and Aaron Shraberg, "The Rise of Chinese Civil-Military Integration" in Tai Ming Cheung, ed., *Forging China's Military Might: A New Framework for Assessing Innovation* (Baltimore, MD: Johns Hopkins University Press, 2014).
- Matthew Luce, "A Model Company: CETC Celebrates 10 Years of Civil-Military Integration," *Jamestown Foundation China Brief*, Vol. 12, No. 4, February 21, 2012.

"System of Systems Operations" (体系作战) and ***"Integrated Joint Operations"*** (一体化联合作战): The PLA's description for how it plans to fight in the future under "informatized conditions" is described in these two phrases: "System of Systems Operations" and "Integrated Joint Operations." They describe PLA aspirations for joint operations enabled by information technology that allow horizontal coordination at lower levels as well as a "plug-and-play" approach for matching different capabilities across the services into a single unit tailored campaign objectives.

- Kevin McCauley, "Quality Over Quantity: A New PLA Modernization Methodology?," *Jamestown Foundation China Brief*, Vol. 14, No. 14, July 17, 2014.
- Kevin McCauley, "System of Systems Operational Capability: Key Supporting Concepts for Future Joint Operations," *Jamestown Foundation China Brief*, Vol. 12, No. 19, October 5, 2012.
- Christopher Twomey, "What's in a Name: Building Anti-Access/Area-Denial Capabilities without Anti-Access/Area-Denial Doctrine," in Roy Kamphausen, David Lai, and Travis Tanner, eds., *Assessing the People's Liberation Army in the Hu Jintao Era* (Carlisle, PA: Army War College Strategic Studies Institute, 2014) <http://www.strategicstudiesinstitute.army.mil/pubs/display.cfm?pubID=1201>.

"Integrated Air and Space [Aerospace] Operations" (空天一体): This is the long-term PLAAF development concept, first discussed in 2004 along with "integrated information and firepower operations" (*xinxi huoli yiti*, 信息火力一体). Instead of the typical U.S. description of air and space as separate domains, the PLAAF has articulated an ambitious concept that defines air and space as a single domain. The concept potentially leads to bureaucratic competition over China's space capabilities, because of the Second Artillery's role in traditional aerospace missions.

- Mark Stokes, "China's Question for Joint Aerospace Power: Concepts and Future of Aspirations," in Richard P. Hallion, Roger Cliff, and Phillip C. Saunders, eds., *The Chinese Air Force: Evolving Concepts, Roles, and Capabilities* (Washington, DC: National Defense University,

Institute for National Strategic Studies, 2012), 33–70 <http://www.ndu.edu/press/lib/pdf/books/chinese-air-force.pdf>.

- Kevin Pollpeter, "The PLAAF and the Integration of Air and Space Power," in Richard P. Hallion, Roger Cliff, and Phillip C. Saunders, eds., *The Chinese Air Force: Evolving Concepts, Roles, and Capabilities* (Washington, DC: National Defense University, Institute for National Strategic Studies, 2012), 165–187.

"Integrated Network Electronic Warfare" **(网电一体战):** This concept describes the coordinated use of electronic, cyber, and space warfare to degrade an enemy's C4ISR capabilities. Developed by General Dai Qingmin, the director of the Fourth Department of the PLA General Staff Department in the early 2000s, integrated network electronic warfare focuses on disrupting an opponent's networks and establishing information dominance. For comparative reference, the Soviet concept of Radio Electronic Combat is probably the closest parallel to Chinese thinking.

- Bryan Krekel, Patton Adams, and George Bakos, *Occupying the Information High Ground: Chinese Capabilities for Computer Network Operations and Cyber Espionage*, U.S.-China Security and Economic Review Commission (March 7, 2012) <http://www.uscc.gov/Research/occupying-information-high-ground-chinese-capabilities-computer-network-operations-and>.

- Timothy L. Thomas, *Decoding The Virtual Dragon - Critical Evolutions In The Science And Philosophy Of China's Information Operations And Military Strategy - The Art Of War And IW* (Ft. Leavenworth, KS: U.S. Foreign Military Studies Office, 2007).

Officer Grades **(职务等级):** Although the point should be self-evident by now, the PLA functions differently than its Western counterparts. The PLA has ten ranks, but 15 grades that denote whether the officer is a leader or a deputy leader at particular level. The grade, not the rank, is the key indicator of authority and position within the PLA. Grade also applies to units, and, for the PLAN, each ship and submarine has a unit grade. The grade level determines who can give orders to whom, and, therefore, grade shapes all joint and combined arms operations within the PLA. The best explanations of officer grades can be found in these two works and the forthcoming *PLA as Organization v2.0*:

- *China's Navy 2007* (Washington, DC: Office of Naval Intelligence, 2007), 2–4 <http://fas.org/irp/agency/oni/chinanavy2007.pdf>.
- Jeffrey Becker, David Liebenberg, and Peter Mackenzie, *Behind the Periscope: Leadership in China's Navy* (Alexandria, VA: CNA Corporation, 2013), 229–232 <http://www.cna.org/research/2013/behind-periscope>.
- Kevin Pollpeter and Kenneth Allen, eds., *PLA as Organization v2.0* (Vienna, VA: Defense Group Inc., Forthcoming 2015), 10–15.

Here are some samples of PLA analysis using grade as the basis for assessment:

- Kenneth Allen, "Assessing the PLA's Promotion Ladder to CMC Member Based on Grades vs. Ranks – Part 1," *Jamestown Foundation China Brief*, Vol. 10, No. 15, July 22, 2010.
- Kenneth Allen, "Assessing the PLA's Promotion Ladder to CMC Member Based on Grades vs. Ranks – Part 2," *Jamestown Foundation China Brief*, Vol. 10, No. 16, August 5, 2010.
- Kenneth Allen and Aaron Shraberg, "Assessing the Grade Structure for China's Aircraft Carriers - Part 1," *Jamestown Foundation China Brief*, Vol. 11, No. 13, July 15, 2011.
- Kenneth Allen and Aaron Shraberg, "Assessing the Grade Structure for China's Aircraft Carriers - Part 2," *Jamestown Foundation China Brief*, Vol. 11, No. 14, July 29, 2011.
- David Chen, "The PLA's Evolving Joint Task Force Structure: Implications for the Aircraft Carrier," *Jamestown Foundation China Brief*, Vol. 11, No. 20, October 28, 2011.

Appendix 5: The PLA Watchers

Below is a select list of PLA specialists who regularly publish analysis of Chinese military and security affairs. The list is by no means exhaustive, but the names and their affiliations will serve as roadmap for the PLA-watching community. There are a number of names missing from this list, but they have been omitted because of their relatively low public profile either in government or the defense contracting community.

Kenneth Allen
Defense Group Inc.

Martin Andrew
GI Zhou Newsletter

Thomas Bickford
CNA Corporation

Richard Bitzinger
Nanyang Tech. University

Dennis J. Blasko
Independent Researcher

Dan Blumenthal
American Enterprise Institute

Michael Chase
RAND Corporation

Andrei Chang
Kanwa Defense Review

Dean Cheng
The Heritage Foundation

Tai Ming Cheung
UC San Diego

Thomas Christensen
Princeton University

Ron Christman
U.S. Department of Defense

Roger Cliff
Atlantic Council

Bernard "Bud" Cole
National War College

J. Michael Cole
Thinking Taiwan Foundation

Cortez Cooper
RAND Corporation

John F. Corbett, Jr.
CENTRA Technology

Jacqueline Deal (nee Newmyer)
Long-Term Strategy Group

Arthur Ding
National Cheng-chi University

Ian Easton
Project 2049 Institute

Andrew S. Erickson
U.S. Naval War College

David Finkelstein
CNA Corporation

Richard Fisher, Jr.
IASC

M. Taylor Fravel
MIT

Aaron Friedberg
Princeton University

Kristen Gunness
RAND and Vantage Point Asia

Michael Glosny
U.S. Naval Post-Graduate School

Lyle Goldstein
U.S. Naval War College

Paul H.B. Godwin
Independent Researcher

Scott W. Harold
RAND Corporation

Daniel Hartnett
CNA Corporation

Timothy Heath
RAND Corporation

Lonnie Henley
Department of Defense

Harlan Jencks
Lawrence Livermore Nat'l. Lab

You Ji
University of New South Wales

Roy Kamphausen
Nat'l. Bureau of Asian Research

APPENDIX 5

Taeho Kim
Hallym University

Maryanne Kivlehan-Wise
CNA Corporation

Daniel Kostecka
Office of Naval Intelligence

David Lai
U.S. Army War College

Kevin Lanzit
Alion Science and Technology

Thomas Mahnken
U.S. Naval War College

Oriana Skylar Mastro
Georgetown University

Kevin McCauley
Independent Analyst

Michael McDevitt
CNA Corporation

Frank Miller
Department of Defense

Wendell Minnick
Defense News

James Mulvenon
Defense Group Inc.

William S. Murray
U.S. Naval War College

Edward O'Dowd
Marine Corps University

Ronald O'Rourke
Congressional Research Service

Michael Pillsbury
Hudson Institute

Kevin Pollpeter
UC San Diego

Susan Puska
Kanava International

Phillip Saunders
National Defense University

Andrew Scobell
RAND Corporation

PLA WATCHERS

David Shambaugh
George Washington University

David Shlapak
RAND Corporation

Mark Stokes
Project 2049 Institute

Michael Swaine
CEIP

Murray Scot Tanner
CNA Corporation

Christopher Twomey
U.S. Naval Post-Graduate School

Wayne Ulman
U.S. Pacific Command

Toshi Yoshihara
U.S. Naval War College

Albert Willner
CNA Corporation

Larry Wortzel
USCC

Shinji Yamaguchi
Nat'l Institute of Defense Studies

Yuan Jingdong
University of Sydney

Christopher Yung
National Defense University

Zhang Xiaoming
Air War College

APPENDIX 6: SELECT PLA AND CHINESE SECURITY BIBLIOGRAPHY

This appendix includes key books and journal articles on Chinese security policymaking, the PLA and its constituent elements, the PLA conference volumes, and useful Congressional Research Service reports.

Background Texts on National Security and Foreign Policymaking

- Mark Burles and Abram Shulsky, *Patterns in China's Use of Force: Evidence from History and Doctrinal Writings* (Santa Monica, CA: RAND, 2000)
  <http://www.rand.org/pubs/monograph_reports/MR1160.html>.

- Chen Jian, *China's Road to the Korean War: The Making of Sino-American Confrontation* (New York: Columbia University Press, 1996).

- Thomas J. Christensen, "Posing Problems without Catching Up: China's Rise and Challenges for U.S. Security Policy," *International Security*, Vol. 25, No. 4 (Spring 2001), 5–40.

- Bruce Elleman, *Modern Chinese Warfare, 1795–1989* (New York: Routledge, 2001).

- M. Taylor Fravel, *Strong Borders, Secure Nation: Cooperation and Conflict in China's Territorial Disputes* (Princeton: Princeton University Press, 2008).

- M. Taylor Fravel, "Power Shifts and Escalation: Explaining Chinas Use of Force in Territorial Disputes," *International Security*, Vol. 32, No. 3 (Winter 2007/2008), 44–83.

- Paul H.B. Godwin and Alice L. Miller, *China's Forbearance Has Limits: Chinese Threat and Retaliation Signaling and Its Implications for a Sino-American Military Confrontation*, China Strategic Perspectives No. 6 (Washington, DC: National Defense University Institute for National Strategic Studies, 2013).

- Timothy Heath, "What Does China Want? Discerning the PRC's National Strategy," *Asian Security* Vol. 8, No. 1 (2012), 54–72.

- Alastair Iain Johnston, *Cultural Realism: Strategic Culture and Grand Strategy in Chinese History* (Princeton, NJ: Princeton University Press, 1998).

- Alistair Iain Johnston, "China's Militarized Interstate Dispute Behavior: A First Cut at the Data," *The China Quarterly*, No. 153 (March 1998), 1–30.

- David M. Lampton, ed., *The Making of Chinese Foreign and Security Policy in the Era of Reform, 1978–2000* (Stanford, CA: Stanford University Press, 2001).

- John Lewis and Xue Litai, *Imagined Enemies: China Prepares for Uncertain War* (Stanford: Stanford University Press, 2008).

- Lu Ning, *The Dynamics of Foreign Policymaking in China* (Boulder, CO: Westview Press, 2000).

- Andrew Nathan and Andrew Scobell, *China's Search for Security* (New York: Columbia University Press, 2012).

- Michael Pillsbury, ed., *Chinese Views of Future Warfare* (Washington, DC: National Defense University Press, 1998) <http://www.au.af.mil/au/awc/awcgate/ndu/chinview/chinacont.html>.

- Michael Pillsbury, *China Debates the Future Security Environment* (Washington, DC: National Defense University Press, 2000).

- Michael Swaine, *The Role of the Chinese Military in National Security Policymaking* (Santa Monica, CA: RAND, 1998) <http://www.rand.org/pubs/monograph_reports/MR782-1.html>.

- Mark Ryan, David Finkelstein, and Michael McDevitt, eds., *Chinese Warfighting: The PLA Experience since 1949* (Armonk, NY: M.E. Sharpe, 2003).

- Andrew Scobell, *China's Use of Military Force: Beyond the Great Wall and the Long March* (Cambridge: Cambridge University Press, 2003).

APPENDIX 6

- Gerald Segal, *Defending China* (New York: Oxford University Press, 1985).

- Allen Whiting, "China's Use of Force, 1950–1996, and Taiwan," *International Security*, Vol. 26, No. 2 (Autumn 2001), 103–131.

The People's Liberation Army - General

- Martin Andrew, *Tuo Mao: The Operational History of the People's Liberation Army*, Ph.D. Dissertation, Bond University (2008) <http://epublications.bond.edu.au/theses/24>.

- Dennis J. Blasko, *The Chinese Army Today: Tradition and Transformation for the 21st Century*, 2nd Edition (New York: Routledge, 2012).

- Dennis J. Blasko, "'Technology Determines Tactics': The Relationship between Technology and Doctrine in Chinese Military Thinking," *Journal of Strategic Studies*, Vol. 34, No. 3 (June 2011), 355–381.

- Michael S. Chase, Jeffrey Engstrom, Tai Ming Cheung, Kristen Gunness, Scott Warren Harold, Susan Puska, and Samuel Berkowitz, *China's Incomplete Military Transformation: Assessing the Weaknesses of the People's Liberation Army (PLA)* (Washington, DC: RAND and U.S.-China Security and Economic Review Commission, 2015) <http://www.uscc.gov/Research/china%E2%80%99s-incomplete-military-transformation-assessing-weaknesses-people%E2%80%99s-liberation-army>.

- Stephen J. Flanagan and Michael E. Marti, eds., *The People's Liberation Army and China in Transition* (Washington, DC: National Defense University, Institute for National Strategic Studies, 2003) <http://www.isn.ethz.ch/Digital-Library/Publications/Detail/?id=100711&lng=en>.

- M. Taylor Fravel, "China's Search for Military Power," *The Washington Quarterly*, Vol. 33, No. 3 (Summer 2008), 125–141.

- Adam P. Liff and Andrew S. Erickson, "Demystifying China's Defence Spending: Less Mysterious in the Aggregate," *The China Quarterly*, No. 216 (December 2013), 805–830.

- Joe McReynolds, ed., *China's Evolving Military Strategy* (Washington, DC: The Jamestown Foundation, 2015).

- James Mulvenon and Andrew N.D. Yang, eds., *Seeking Truth From Facts: A Retrospective on Chinese Military Studies in the Post-Mao Era* (Santa Monica, CA: RAND, 2001) <http://www.rand.org/pubs/conf_proceedings/CF160.html>.

- James Mulvenon and Andrew N.D. Yang, eds., *The People's Liberation Army as Organization: Reference Volume 1.0* (Santa Monica, CA: RAND, 2002) <http://www.rand.org/pubs/conf_proceedings/CF182.html>.

- James Mulvenon and David Finkelstein, eds., *China's Revolution in Doctrinal Affairs: Emerging Trends in the Operational Art of the Chinese People's Liberation Army* (Alexandria, VA: CNA Corporation and Defense Group Inc., 2005) <https://www.cna.org/research/2005/chinas-revolution-doctrinal-affairs>.

- Ka Po Ng, *Interpreting China's Military Power: Doctrine Makes Readiness* (New York: Frank Cass, 2005).

- Edward O'Dowd, *Chinese Military Strategy in the Third Indochina War: The Last Maoist War* (New York: Routledge, 2007).

- David Shambaugh, *Modernizing China's Military: Progress, Problems, and Prospects* (Berkeley, CA: University of California Press, 2003).

- Ashley J. Tellis and Travis Tanner, eds., *Strategic Asia 2012–13: China's Military Challenge* (Seattle, WA: The National Bureau of Asian Research, 2012).

- Yao Yunzhu, "The Evolution of Military Doctrine of the Chinese PLA from 1985 to 1995," *Korean Journal of Defense Analysis*, Vol. 7, No. 2 (1995), 57–80.

APPENDIX 6

Organizational Basics

- Dennis J. Blasko, *The Chinese Army Today: Tradition and Transformation for the 21st Century*, 2nd Edition (New York: Routledge, 2012).
- *China's Navy 2007* (Washington, DC: Office of Naval Intelligence, 2007) <http://fas.org/irp/agency/oni/chinanavy2007.pdf>.
- James Mulvenon and Andrew N.D. Yang, eds., *The People's Liberation Army as Organization: Reference Volume 1.0* (Santa Monica, CA: RAND, 2002) <http://www.rand.org/pubs/conf_proceedings/CF182.html>.
- *People's Liberation Army Air Force 2010* (Wright-Patterson AFB, OH: National Air and Space Intelligence Center, 2010) <http://www.au.af.mil/au/awc/awcgate/nasic/pla_af_2010.pdf>.
- Kevin Pollpeter and Kenneth Allen, eds., *PLA as Organization v2.0* (Vienna, VA: Defense Group Inc., Forthcoming 2015).

The PLA Ground Forces

- Dennis J. Blasko, *The Chinese Army Today: Tradition and Transformation for the 21st Century*, 2nd Edition (New York: Routledge, 2012).
- Xiaobing Li, *A History of the Modern Chinese Army* (Lexington, KY: The University Press of Kentucky, 2007).

The PLA Air Force

- Kenneth W. Allen, *The Ten Pillars of the People's Liberation Army Air Force: An Assessment*, The Jamestown Foundation, Occasional Paper (2011).
- Kenneth W. Allen, Glenn Krumel, and Jonathan Pollack, *The PLA Air Force Enters the 21st Century* (Santa Monica, CA: RAND, 1995) <http://www.rand.org/pubs/monograph_reports/MR580.html>.

- Richard Bueschel, *Chinese Communist Air Power* (New York: Praeger, 1968).

- Roger Cliff, John F. Fei, Jeff Hagen, Elizabeth Hague, Eric Heginbotham, and John Stillion, *Shaking the Heavens and Splitting the Earth: Chinese Air Force Employment Concepts in the 21st Century* (Santa Monica, CA: RAND, 2011) <http://www.rand.org/pubs/monographs/MG915.html>.

- Richard P. Hallion, Roger Cliff, and Phillip C. Saunders, eds., *The Chinese Air Force: Evolving Concepts, Roles, and Capabilities* (Washington, DC: National Defense University, Institute for National Strategic Studies, 2012) <http://ndupress.ndu.edu/Portals/68/Documents/Books/chinese-air-force.pdf>.

- *People's Liberation Army Air Force 2010* (Wright-Patterson AFB, OH: National Air and Space Intelligence Center, 2010) <http://www.au.af.mil/au/awc/awcgate/nasic/pla_af_2010.pdf>.

- Xiaoming Zhang, *Red Wings over the Yalu: China, the Soviet Union, and the Air War in Korea* (College Station, TX: Texas A&M University Press, 2003).

The PLA Navy

- Jeffrey Becker, David Liebenberg, and Peter Mackenzie, *Behind the Periscope: Leadership in China's Navy* (Alexandria, VA: CNA Corporation, 2013) <http://www.cna.org/research/2013/behind-periscope>.

- Bernard D. Cole, *The Great Wall at Sea: China's Navy Enters the Twenty-First Century*, 2nd Edition (Annapolis, MD: Naval Institute Press, 2012).

- Andrew S. Erickson, Lyle J. Goldstein, Andrew R. Wilson, and William S. Murray, eds., *China's Future Nuclear Submarine Force* (Annapolis, MD: Naval Institute Press, 2007).

- Andrew S. Erickson, "Rising Tides, Dispersing Waves: Opportunities and Challenges in Chinese Seapower Development," *Journal of Strategic Studies*, Vol. 37, No. 3 (2014), 372–402.

- Gao Xiaoxing, *The PLA Navy* (Beijing: CN Times Books, 2014).

- James Holmes and Toshi Yoshihara, *Chinese Naval Strategy in the 21st Century: The Turn to Mahan* (New York: Routledge, 2012).

- Phillip C. Saunders, Christopher D. Yung, Michael Swaine and Andrew Nien-Dzu Yang, eds., *The Chinese Navy: Expanding Capabilities, Evolving Roles* (Washington, DC: National Defense University Press, 2011) <http://www.ndu.edu/press/lib/pdf/books/chinese-navy.pdf>.

- *China's Navy 2007* (Washington, DC: Office of Naval Intelligence, 2007) <http://fas.org/irp/agency/oni/chinanavy2007.pdf>.

- *The PLA Navy: New Capabilities and Missions for the 21st Century* (Washington, DC: Office of Naval Intelligence, 2015) <http://www.oni.navy.mil/Intelligence_Community/china.html>.

- *The People's Liberation Army Navy: A Modern Navy with Chinese Characteristics* (Washington, DC: Office of Naval Intelligence, 2009) <http://www.oni.navy.mil/Intelligence_Community/docs/china_army_navy.pdf>.

China's Rocket Forces: The Second Artillery

- Michael S. Chase and Andrew S. Erickson, "The Conventional Missile Capabilities of China's Second Artillery Force: Cornerstone of Deterrence and Warfighting," *Asian Security*, Vol. 8, No. 2 (2012), 115–137.

- Ron Christman, "Conventional Missions for China's Second Artillery Corps," *Comparative Strategy*, Vol. 30, No. 3 (2011), 198–228.

- *Ballistic and Cruise Missile Threat* (Wright-Patterson AFB, OH: National Air and Space Intelligence Center, 2013)

<http://fas.org/programs/ssp/nukes/nuclearweapons/NASIC2013_050813.pdf>.

- Michael Chase, Andrew S. Erickson, and Christopher Yeaw, "Chinese Theater and Strategic Missile Force Modernization and its Implications for the United States," *Journal of Strategic Studies*, Vol. 32, No. 1 (February 2009), 67–114.

- Dennis M. Gormley, Andrew S. Erickson, and Jingdong Yuan, *A Low-Visibility Force Multiplier: Assessing China's Cruise Missile Ambitions* (Washington, D.C.: National Defense University Press, 2014) <http://ndupress.ndu.edu/portals/68/documents/books/force-multiplier.pdf>.

- Mark Stokes, *China's Strategic Modernization: Implications for the United States* (Carlisle, PA: Army War College Strategic Studies Institute, 1999).

Chinese Nuclear Forces

- Ta-chen Cheng, "China's Nuclear Command, Control, and Operations," *International Relations of the Asia-Pacific*, Vol. 7, No. 2 (2007), 155–178.

- Thomas J. Christensen, "The Meaning of the Nuclear Evolution: China's Strategic Modernization and US-China Security Relations," *Journal of Strategic Studies*, Vol. 35, No. 4 (Fall 2012), 447–487.

- M. Taylor Fravel and Evan Medeiros, "China's Search for Assured Retaliation," *International Security*, Vol. 35, No. 2 (Spring 2006), 48–87.

- Alastair Iain Johnston, "China's New 'Old Thinking': The Concept of Limited Deterrence," *International Security*, Vol. 20, No. 3 (1996), 5–42.

- Jeffrey Lewis, *The Minimum Means of Reprisal: China's Search for Security in the Nuclear Age* (Cambridge, MA: The MIT Press, 2007).

- Jeffrey Lewis, "China's Nuclear Modernization: Surprise, Restraint, and Uncertainty," in Ashley J. Tellis, Abraham M. Denmark and Travis Tanner, eds., *Strategic Asia 2013–14: Asia in the Second Nuclear*

Age (Seattle, WA: The National Bureau of Asian Research, 2013), 67–97.

- John Lewis and Xue Litai, *China Builds the Bomb* (Stanford, CA: Stanford University Press, 1991).

- Jonathan Ray, *Red China's "Capitalist Bomb": Inside the Chinese Neutron Bomb Program*, China Strategic Perspectives, No. 8 (Washington, DC: National Defense University Institute for National Strategic Studies, 2015).

- Mark Stokes and Ian Easton, *Half Lives: A Preliminary Assessment of China's Nuclear Warhead Life Extension and Safety Program*, Project 2049 Institute, Occasional Paper (July 2013) <http://project2049.net/publications.html>.

- Mark Stokes, *China's Nuclear Warhead Storage and Handling System*, Project 2049 Institute, Occasional Paper (March 2010) <http://project2049.net/publications.html>.

- Larry Wortzel, *China's Nuclear Forces: Operations, Training, Doctrine, Command, Control and Campaign Planning* (Carlisle, PA: Army War College Strategic Studies Institute, 2007) <http://www.strategicstudiesinstitute.army.mil/pubs/display.cfm?pubID=776>.

- Wu Riqiang, "Certainty of Uncertainty: Nuclear Strategy with Chinese Characteristics," *Journal of Strategic Studies*, Vol. 36, No. 4 (Spring 2013), 579–614.

Civil-Military Relations

- David M. Finkelstein and Kristen Gunness, eds., *Civil-Military Relations in Today's China: Swimming in a New Sea* (New York: Routledge, 2007).

- Timothy Heath, "Toward Strategic Leadership: Chinese Communist Party People's Liberation Army Relations in the Hu Era," in Roy Kamphausen, David Lai, and Travis Tanner, eds., *Assessing the People's*

Liberation Army in the Hu Jintao Era (Carlisle, PA: Army War College Strategic Studies Institute, 2014), 399–440.

- Harlan W. Jencks, *From Muskets to Missiles: Politics and Professionalism in the Chinese Army, 1945–1981* (Boulder, CO: Westview Press, 1982).

- Ellis Joffe, *Party and Army: Professionalism and Political Control in the Chinese Officer Corps, 1949–1964* (Cambridge, MA: Harvard East Asian Monographs, 1967).

- Ellis Joffe, *The Chinese Army after Mao* (Cambridge, MA: Harvard University Press, 1987).

- Michael Kiselycznyk and Phillip C. Saunders, *Civil-Military Relations in China: Assessing the PLA's Role in Elite Politics*, Institute for National Strategic Studies, China Strategic Perspectives No. 2 (August 2010).

- Nan Li, ed., *Chinese Civil-Military Relations: The Transformation of the People's Liberation Army* (New York: Routledge, 2006).

- Yawei Liu and Justine Zheng Ren, "An Emerging Consensus on the U.S. Threat: The United States According to PLA Officers," *Journal of Contemporary China*, Vol. 23, No. 86 (2014), 255–274.

- Andrew Scobell, "China's Evolving Civil- Military Relations: Creeping Guojiahua," *Armed Forces and Society*, Vol. 31, No. 2 (Winter 2005), 227–244.

- Michael Swaine, *The Military and Political Succession in China: Leadership, Institutions, Beliefs* (Santa Monica, CA: RAND, 1992) <http://www.rand.org/pubs/reports/R4254.html>.

- William W. Whitson with Chen-hsia Huang, *The Chinese High Command: A History of Communist Military Politics, 1927–71* (New York: Praeger Publishers, 1973).

- You Ji and Daniel Alderman, "Changing Civil-Military Relations in China," in Roy Kamphausen, David Lai, and Andrew Scobell, eds., *The PLA at Home and Abroad: Assessing the Operational Capabilities of China's Military* (Carlisle, PA: Army War College Strategic Studies Institute, 2010), 135–192.

China's Defense-Industrial Base

- Mikhail Barabanov, Vasiliy Kashin, and Konstantin Makienko, *Shooting Star: China's Military Machine in the 21st Century* (Minneapolis, MN: East View Press, 2012).

- Richard A. Bitzinger, "China's Defense Technology and Industrial Base in a Regional Context: Arms Manufacturing in Asia," *Journal of Strategic Studies*, Vol. 34, No. 3 (June 2011), 425–450.

- Tai Ming Cheung, "The Chinese Defense Economy's Long March from Imitation to Innovation," *Journal of Strategic Studies*, Vol. 34, No. 3 (June 2011), 325–354.

- Tai Ming Cheung, "Dragon on the Horizon: China's Defense Industrial Renaissance," *Journal of Strategic Studies*, Vol. 32, No. 1 (2009), 29–66.

- Tai Ming Cheung, *Fortifying China: The Struggle to Build a Modern Defense Economy* (Ithaca, NY: Cornell University Press, 2009).

- Tai Ming Cheung, ed., *Forging China's Military Might: A New Framework for Assessing Innovation* (Baltimore, MD: Johns Hopkins University Press, 2014).

- Roger Cliff, Chad J. R. Ohlandt, and David Yang, *Ready for Takeoff: China's Advancing Aerospace Industry* (Santa Monica, CA: RAND, 2011) <http://www.rand.org/pubs/monographs/MG1100.html>.

- Evan Feigenbaum, *China's Techno-Warriors: National Security and Strategic Competition from the Nuclear to the Information Age* (Stanford: Stanford University Press, 2003).

- Paul H.B. Godwin, ed., *The Chinese Defense Establishment: Continuity and Change in the 1980s* (Boulder, CO: Westview Press, 1983).

- William C. Hannas, James Mulvenon, and Anna B. Puglisi, *Chinese Industrial Espionage: Technology Acquisition and Military Modernization* (New York: Routledge, 2013).

- Evan Medeiros, Roger Cliff, Keith Crane, and James Mulvenon, *A New Direction for China's Defense Industry* (Santa Monica, CA: RAND, 2005) <http://www.rand.org/pubs/monographs/MG334.html>.
- Kevin Pollpeter, ed., *Getting to Innovation: Assessing China's Defense Research, Development, and Acquisition System* (La Jolla, CA: University of California Institute on Global Conflict and Cooperation, January 2014) <http://igcc.ucsd.edu/assets/001/505308.pdf>.
- Gerald Segal and Richard H. Yang, eds., *Chinese Economic Reform: The Impact on Security* (London: Routledge, 1996).

China-Taiwan Military Balance

- Richard Bush and Michael O'Hanlon, *A War Like No Other: The Truth about China's Challenge to America* (Hoboken, NJ: John Wiley & Sons, 2007).
- Dean Cheng, *Taiwan's Maritime Security: A Critical American Interest*, The Heritage Foundation, Backgrounder No. 2889, March 19, 2014 <http://www.heritage.org/research/reports/2014/03/taiwans-maritime-security-a-critical-american-interest>.
- Roger Cliff, Phillip C. Saunders, and Scott Harold, eds., *New Opportunities and Challenges for Taiwan's Security* (Santa Monica, CA: RAND, 2011) <http://www.rand.org/pubs/conf_proceedings/CF279.html>.
- Ian Easton, *Able Archers: Taiwan Defense Strategy in an Age of Precision Strike*, Project 2049 Institute, Occasional Paper (September 2014) <http://project2049.net/publications.html>.
- Michael Glosny, "Strangulation from the Sea: A PRC Submarine Blockade of Taiwan," *International Security*, Vol. 28, No. 4 (Spring 2004), 125–160.
- William S. Murray, "Revisiting Taiwan's Defense Strategy," *Naval War College Review*, Vol. 61, No. 3 (Summer 2008), 13–38.

APPENDIX 6

- Michael O'Hanlon, "Why China Cannot Conquer Taiwan," *International Security*, Vol. 25, No. 2 (Fall 2000), 51–86.

- James Lilley and Chuck Downs, eds., *Crisis in the Taiwan Strait* (Washington, DC: National Defense University and the American Enterprise Institute, 1997).

- ROC Ministry of National Defense [Taiwan], *Quadrennial Defense Review 2013* <http://qdr.mnd.gov.tw/encontent.html>.

- ROC Ministry of National Defense [Taiwan], *National Defense Report 2013* <http://report.mnd.gov.tw/index.html>.

- Robert Ross, "Navigating the Taiwan Strait: Deterrence, Escalation Dominance, and U.S.-China Relations," *International Security*, Vol. 27, No. 2 (Fall 2002), 48–85.

- David Shambaugh, "A Matter of Time: Taiwan's Eroding Military Advantage," *The Washington Quarterly*, Vol. 23, No. 2 (2000), 119–133.

- David A. Shlapak, David T. Orletsky, Toy I. Reid, Murray Scot Tanner, and Barry Wilson, *A Question of Balance: Political Context and Military Aspects of the China-Taiwan Dispute* (Santa Monica, CA: RAND, 2009) <http://www.rand.org/pubs/monographs/MG888.html>.

- Michael Swaine, Andrew N.D. Yang, and Evan Medeiros with Oriana Skylar Mastro, eds., *Assessing the Threat: The Chinese Military and Taiwan's Security* (Washington, DC: Carnegie Endowment for International Peace, 2007).

Chinese Cyber, Information Operations, and Intelligence

- Greg Austin, *Cyber Policy in China* (Cambridge: Polity Press, 2014).

- Amy Chang, *Warring State: China's Cybersecurity Strategy*, Center for a New American Security, December 3, 2014 <http://www.cnas.org/chinas-cybersecurity-strategy#.VPejUfmUc_Y>.

- William C. Hannas, James Mulvenon, and Anna B. Puglisi, *Chinese Industrial Espionage: Technology Acquisition and Military Modernization* (New York: Routledge, 2013).
- Nigel Inkster, "China in Cyberspace," *Survival*, Vol. 52, No. 4 (August 2010), 55–66.
- Bryan Krekel, Patton Adams, and George Bakos, *Occupying the Information High Ground: Chinese Capabilities for Computer Network Operations and Cyber Espionage*, Report for the U.S.-China Security and Economic Review Commission, March 8, 2012 <http://origin.www.uscc.gov/sites/default/files/Research/USCC_Report_Chinese_Capabilities_for_Computer_Network_Operations_and_Cyber_%20Espionage.pdf>.
- Jon Lindsay, Tai Ming Cheung, and Derek Reveron, eds., *China and Cybersecurity: Espionage, Strategy, and Politics in the Digital Domain* (Oxford: Oxford University Press, 2015).
- Peter Mattis, "Assessing Western Perspectives on Chinese Intelligence," *International Journal of Intelligence and Counterintelligence*, Vol. 25, No. 4 (September 2012), 678–699.
- Peter Mattis, "Beyond Spy vs. Spy: The Analytic Challenge of Understanding Chinese Intelligence Services," *Studies in Intelligence*, Vol. 56, No. 3 (September 2012), 47–57.
- James Mulvenon, "PLA Computer Network Operations: Scenarios, Doctrine, Organizations, and Capability," in Roy Kamphausen, David Lai, and Andrew Scobell, eds., *Beyond the Strait: PLA Missions Beyond Taiwan* (Carlisle, PA: Army War College Strategic Studies Institute, 2009), 253–286.
- Mark A. Stokes, Jenny Lin and L.C. Russell Hsiao, *The Chinese People's Liberation Army Signals Intelligence and Cyber Reconnaissance Infrastructure*, Project 2049 Institute, November 11, 2011 <http://project2049.net/documents/pla_third_department_sigint_cyber_stokes_lin_hsiao.pdf>.

APPENDIX 6

- Timothy L. Thomas, *Decoding The Virtual Dragon - Critical Evolutions In The Science And Philosophy Of China's Information Operations And Military Strategy - The Art Of War And IW* (Ft. Leavenworth, KS: U.S. Foreign Military Studies Office, 2007).

China Space Issues and Space-Based Capabilities

- Dean Cheng, *China's Space Program: A Growing Factor in U.S. Security Planning*, The Heritage Foundation, Backgrounder No. 2594, August 16, 2011 <http://www.heritage.org/research/reports/2011/08/chinas-space-program-a-growing-factor-in-us-security-planning>.

- Dean Cheng, "China's Military Role in Space," *Strategic Studies Quarterly*, Vol. 6, No. 1 (Spring 2012), 55–77 <http://www.au.af.mil/au/ssq/2012/spring/cheng.pdf>.

- Dean Cheng and Mark Stokes, *China's Evolving Space Capabilities: Implications for U.S. Interests*, Report for U.S.-China Security and Economic Review Commission, April 26, 2012 <http://www.uscc.gov/Research/chinas-evolving-space-capabilities-implications-us-interests>.

- Ian Easton, *The Great Game in Space: China's Evolving ASAT Weapons Programs and Their Implications for Future U.S. Strategy*, Project 2049 Institute, Occasional Paper (June 2009) <http://project2049.net/publications.html>.

- Ian Easton, *China's Evolving Reconnaissance-Strike Capabilities: Implications for the U.S.-Japan Alliance*, Project 2049 Institute, Occasional Paper (February 2014) <http://project2049.net/publications.html>.

- Eric Hagt and Matthew Durnin, "Space: China's Tactical Frontier," *Journal of Strategic Studies*, Vol. 34, No. 5 (2011), 733–761.

- Michael Krepon and Julia Thompson, eds., *Anti-Satellite Weapons, Deterrence, and Sino-American Space Relations* (Washington, DC: Stimson Center, 2013) <http://www.stimson.org/program-news/krepon-

and-thompson-on-anti-satellite-weapons-deterrence-and-sino-american-space-relations>.

- Michael Krepon, Eric Hagt, Shen Dingli, Bao Shixiu, Michael Pillsbury, and Ashley Tellis, "China's Space Strategy: An Exchange," *Survival*, Vol. 50, No. 1 (2008), 157–198.

- Kevin Pollpeter, "Upward and Onward: Technological Innovation and Organizational Change in China's Space Industry," *Journal of Strategic Studies*, Vol. 34, No. 3 (2011), 405–423.

- Kevin Pollpeter, Eric Anderson, Jordan Wilson, and Fan Yang, *China Dream, Space Dream: China's Progress in Space Technologies and Implications of the United States*, Report for the U.S.-China Security and Economic Review Commission, March 2, 2015 <http://www.uscc.gov/Research/china-dream-space-dream-chinas-progress-space-technologies-and-implications-united-states>.

Annual Army War College-NBR PLA Conference Volumes[79]

- Roy Kamphausen, David Lai, and Travis Tanner, eds., *Assessing the People's Liberation Army in the Hu Jintao Era* (Carlisle, PA: Army War College Strategic Studies Institute, 2014) <http://www.strategicstudiesinstitute.army.mil/pubs/display.cfm?pubID=1201>.

- Travis Tanner, Roy Kamphausen, and David Lai, eds., *Learning by Doing: The PLA Trains at Home and Abroad* (Carlisle, PA: Army War College Strategic Studies Institute, 2012) <http://www.strategicstudiesinstitute.army.mil/pubs/display.cfm?pubID=1135>.

---

[79] The Strategic Studies Institute website is now inaccessible for readers located outside the United States; however, the PDFs also are available in the digital library of The International Relations and Security Network, an online repository of analysis created by the Swiss Federal Institute of Technology Zurich <http://www.isn.ethz.ch>.

APPENDIX 6

- Andrew Scobell, David Lai, and Roy Kamphausen, eds., *Chinese Lessons from Other Peoples' War* (Carlisle, PA: Army War College Strategic Studies Institute, 2011) <http://www.strategicstudiesinstitute.army.mil/pubs/display.cfm?pubID=1090>.

- Roy Kamphausen, David Lai, and Andrew Scobell, eds., *The PLA at Home and Abroad: Assessing the Operational Capabilities of China's Military* (Carlisle, PA: Army War College Strategic Studies Institute, 2010) <http://www.strategicstudiesinstitute.army.mil/pubs/display.cfm?pubID=995>.

- Roy Kamphausen, David Lai, and Andrew Scobell, eds., *Beyond the Strait: PLA Missions Beyond Taiwan* (Carlisle, PA: Army War College Strategic Studies Institute, 2009) <http://www.strategicstudiesinstitute.army.mil/pubs/display.cfm?pubID=910>.

- Roy Kamphausen, Andrew Scobell, and Travis Tanner, eds., *The 'People' in the PLA: Recruitment, Training, and Education in China's Military* (Carlisle, PA: Army War College Strategic Studies Institute, 2008) <http://www.strategicstudiesinstitute.army.mil/pubs/display.cfm?pubID=858>.

- Roy Kamphausen and Andrew Scobell, eds., *Right Sizing the People's Liberation Army: Exploring the Contours of China's Military* (Carlisle, PA: Army War College Strategic Studies Institute, 2007) <http://www.strategicstudiesinstitute.army.mil/pubs/display.cfm?pubID=784>.

- Andrew Scobell and Larry M. Wortzel, eds., *Shaping China's Security Environment: The Role of the People's Liberation Army* (Carlisle, PA: Army War College Strategic Studies Institute, 2006) <http://www.strategicstudiesinstitute.army.mil/pubs/display.cfm?pubID=709>.

- Andrew Scobell and Larry M. Wortzel, eds., *Chinese National Security: Decisionmaking Under Stress* (Carlisle, PA: Army War College Strategic Studies Institute, 2005)

<http://www.strategicstudiesinstitute.army.mil/pubs/display.cfm?pubID=623>.

- Andrew Scobell and Larry M. Wortzel, eds., *Civil-Military Change in China: Elites, Institutes, and Ideas After the 16th Party Congress* (Carlisle, PA: Army War College Strategic Studies Institute, 2004) <http://www.strategicstudiesinstitute.army.mil/pubs/display.cfm?pubID=413>.

- Laurie Burkitt, Andrew Scobell, and Larry M. Wortzel, eds., *The Lessons of History: The Chinese People's Liberation Army at 75* (Carlisle, PA: Army War College Strategic Studies Institute, 2003) <http://www.strategicstudiesinstitute.army.mil/pubs/display.cfm?pubID=52>.

- Andrew Scobell and Larry M. Wortzel, eds., *China's Growing Military Power: Perspectives on Security, Ballistic Missiles, and Conventional Capabilities* (Carlisle, PA: Army War College Strategic Studies Institute, 2002) <http://www.strategicstudiesinstitute.army.mil/pubs/display.cfm?pubID=59>.

- Andrew Scobell, ed., *The Costs of Conflict: The Impact on China of a Future War* (Carlisle, PA: Army War College Strategic Studies Institute, 2001) <http://www.strategicstudiesinstitute.army.mil/pubs/display.cfm?pubID=63>.

- Dennison Lane, Mark Weisenbloom, and Dimon Liu, eds., *Chinese Military Modernization* (Washington, DC: American Enterprise Institute Press, 1996).

U.S. Naval War College China Maritime Studies Institute Volumes

- Andrew S. Erickson and Lyle J. Goldstein, eds., *Chinese Aerospace Power: Evolving Maritime Roles* (Annapolis, MD: Naval Institute Press with the China Maritime Studies Institute, 2011).

- Andrew S. Erickson, Lyle J. Goldstein, and Nan Li, eds., *China, the United States, and 21st-Century Sea Power: Defining a Maritime Security*

Partnership (Annapolis, MD: Naval Institute Press with the China Maritime Studies Institute, 2010).

- Andrew S. Erickson, Lyle J. Goldstein, and Carnes Lord, eds., *China Goes to Sea: Maritime Transformation in Comparative Historical Perspective* (Annapolis, MD: Naval Institute Press with the China Maritime Studies Institute, 2009).

- Gabriel B. Collins, Andrew S. Erickson, Lyle J. Goldstein, and William S. Murray, eds., *China's Energy Strategy: The Impact on Beijing's Maritime Policies* (Annapolis, MD: Naval Institute Press with the China Maritime Studies Institute, 2008).

- Andrew S. Erickson, Lyle J. Goldstein, William S. Murray, and Andrew Wilson, eds., *China's Future Nuclear Submarine Force* (Annapolis, MD: Naval Institute Press with the China Maritime Studies Institute, 2007).

Available CAPS-RAND Conference Volumes

- Richard P. Hallion, Roger Cliff, and Phillip C. Saunders, eds., *The Chinese Air Force: Evolving Concepts, Roles, and Capabilities* (Washington, DC: National Defense University, Institute for National Strategic Studies, 2012) <http://www.ndu.edu/press/lib/pdf/books/chinese-air-force.pdf>.

- Phillip C. Saunders, Christopher D. Yung, Michael Swaine, and Andrew Nien-Dzu Yang, eds., *The Chinese Navy: Expanding Capabilities, Evolving Roles* (Washington, DC: National Defense University Press, 2011) <http://www.ndu.edu/press/lib/pdf/books/chinese-navy.pdf>.

- Roger Cliff, Phillip C. Saunders, and Scott W. Harold, eds., *New Opportunities and Challenges for Taiwan's Security* (Santa Monica, CA: RAND, 2011) <http://www.rand.org/pubs/conf_proceedings/CF279.html>.

- James Mulvenon and Andrew N.D. Yang, eds., *Seeking Truth From Facts: A Retrospective on Chinese Military Studies in the Post-Mao Era* (Santa Monica, CA: RAND, 2004) <http://www.rand.org/pubs/conf_proceedings/CF189.html >.

- James Mulvenon and Andrew N.D. Yang, eds., *The People's Liberation Army as Organization: Reference Volume 1.0* (Santa Monica, CA: RAND, 2002) <http://www.rand.org/pubs/conf_proceedings/CF182.html>.

- James Mulvenon and Andrew N.D. Yang, eds., *Seeking Truth From Facts: A Retrospective on Chinese Military Studies in the Post-Mao Era* (Santa Monica, CA: RAND, 2001) <http://www.rand.org/pubs/conf_proceedings/CF160.html>.

- James Mulvenon and Andrew N.D. Yang, eds., *The People's Liberation Army in the Information Age* (Santa Monica, CA: RAND, 1999) <http://www.rand.org/pubs/conf_proceedings/CF145.html>.

- Jonathan Pollack and Richard H. Yang, eds., *In China's Shadow: Regional Perspectives on Chinese Foreign Policy and Military Development* (Santa Monica, CA: RAND, 1998) <http://www.rand.org/pubs/conf_proceedings/CF137.html>.

Strategic Asia Volumes

- Ashley J. Tellis, Abraham M. Denmark, and Greg Chaffin, *Strategic Asia 2014–15: U.S. Alliances and Partnerships at the Center of Global Power* (Seattle, WA: The National Bureau of Asian Research, 2014).

- Ashley J. Tellis, Abraham M. Denmark, and Travis Tanner, eds., *Strategic Asia 2013–14: Asia in the Second Nuclear Age* (Seattle, WA: The National Bureau of Asian Research, 2013).

- Ashley J. Tellis and Travis Tanner, eds., *Strategic Asia 2012–13: China's Military Challenge* (Seattle, WA: The National Bureau of Asian Research, 2012).

APPENDIX 6

- Ashley J. Tellis, Abraham M. Denmark, and Jessica Keough, eds., *Strategic Asia 2011–12: Asia Responds to Its Rising Powers* (Seattle, WA: The National Bureau of Asian Research, 2011).

- Ashley J. Tellis, Andrew Marble, and Travis Tanner, eds., *Strategic Asia 2010–11: Asia's Rising Power and America's Continued Purpose* (Seattle, WA: The National Bureau of Asian Research, 2010).

- Ashley J. Tellis, Andrew Marble, and Travis Tanner, eds., *Strategic Asia 2009–10: Economic Meltdown and Geopolitical Stability* (Seattle, WA: The National Bureau of Asian Research, 2009).

- Ashley J. Tellis, Mercy Kuo, and Andrew Marble, eds., *Strategic Asia 2008–09: Challenges and Choices* (Seattle, WA: The National Bureau of Asian Research, 2008).

- Ashley J. Tellis and Michael Wills, eds., *Strategic Asia 2007–08: Domestic Political Change and Grand Strategy* (Seattle, WA: The National Bureau of Asian Research, 2007).

- Ashley J. Tellis and Michael Wills, eds., *Strategic Asia 2006–07: Trade, Interdependence, and Security* (Seattle, WA: The National Bureau of Asian Research, 2006).

- Ashley J. Tellis and Michael Wills, eds., *Strategic Asia 2005–06: Military Modernization in the Era of Uncertainty* (Seattle, WA: The National Bureau of Asian Research, 2005).

- Ashley J. Tellis and Michael Wills, eds., *Strategic Asia 2004–05: Confronting Terrorism in the Pursuit of Power* (Seattle, WA: The National Bureau of Asian Research, 2004).

- Richard J. Ellings, Aaron L. Friedberg, and Michael Wills, eds., *Strategic Asia 2003–04: Fragility and Crisis* (Seattle, WA: The National Bureau of Asian Research, 2003).

- Richard J. Ellings, Aaron L. Friedberg, and Michael Wills, eds., *Strategic Asia 2002–03: Asian Aftershocks* (Seattle, WA: The National Bureau of Asian Research, 2002).

- Richard J. Ellings and Aaron L. Friedberg, eds., *Strategic Asia 2001–02: Power and Purpose* (Seattle, WA: The National Bureau of Asian Research, 2001).

Chinese Security- and PLA-Related Congressional Research Service Reports

- Ronald O'Rourke, *China Naval Modernization: Implications for U.S. Navy Capabilities—Background and Issues for Congress*, RL33153, August 5, 2014 <http://fas.org/sgp/crs/row/RL33153.pdf>.

- Ronald O'Rourke, *Maritime Territorial and Exclusive Economic Zone (EEZ) Disputes Involving China: Issues for Congress*, R42784, August 5, 2014 <http://fas.org/sgp/crs/row/R42784.pdf>.

- Shirley A. Kan, *Taiwan: Major U.S. Arms Sales Since 1990*, RL30957, June 13, 2014 <http://fas.org/sgp/crs/weapons/RL30957.pdf>.

- Shirley A. Kan and Wayne M. Morrison, *U.S.-Taiwan Relationship: Overview of Policy Issues*, R41952, April 22, 2014 <http://fas.org/sgp/crs/row/R41952.pdf>.

- Susan V. Lawrence, *China's Political Institutions and Leaders in Charts*, R43303, November 12, 2013 <http://fas.org/sgp/crs/row/R43303.pdf>.

- Susan V. Lawrence, *U.S.-China Relations: An Overview of Policy Issues*, R41108, August 1, 2013 <http://fas.org/sgp/crs/row/R41108.pdf>.

- Susan V. Lawrence and Michael F. Martin, *Understanding China's Political System*, R41007, March 20, 2013 <http://fas.org/sgp/crs/row/R41007.pdf>.

- Shirley A. Kan, *U.S.-China Military Contacts: Issues for Congress*, RL32496, March 19, 2013 <http://www.au.af.mil/au/awc/awcgate/crs/rl32496.pdf>.

APPENDIX 7: THE 1990S REVOLUTION IN THE PLA

The 1990s were a critical time in the modernization of the People's Liberation Army. Below are a few quick citations that go into detail on the dramatic changes and drivers shaping PLA modernization that date to the 1990s. The single best introduction to many of these developments remains, Dennis J. Blasko, *The Chinese Army Today: Tradition and Transformation for the 21st Century*, 2nd Edition (New York: Routledge, 2012).

- **Reforms to Education/Training:** Roy Kamphausen, Andrew Scobell, and Travis Tanner, eds., *The 'People' in the PLA: Recruitment, Training, and Education in China's Military* (Carlisle, PA: Army War College Strategic Studies Institute, 2008).

- **U.S. Victory in the Gulf War:** Dean Cheng, "Chinese Lessons from the Gulf Wars," in Andrew Scobell, David Lai, and Roy Kamphausen, eds., *Chinese Lessons from Other Peoples' War* (Carlisle, PA: Army War College Strategic Studies Institute, 2011).

- **Impact of the Taiwan Strait Crises and the Chinese Embassy Bombing:** Andrew S. Erickson, *Chinese Anti-Ship Ballistic Missile (ASBM) Development: Drivers, Trajectories and Strategic Implications* (Washington, DC: The Jamestown Foundation, 2013).

- **Shifting Roles in Internal Security from the PLA to People's Armed Police:** Tai Ming Cheung, "Guarding China's Domestic Front Line: The People's Armed Police and China's Stability," *The China Quarterly*, No. 146, Special Issue: China's Military in Transition (June 1996), 525–547.

- **Dual-Use Policy in Defense Industries:** Tai Ming Cheung, *Fortifying China: The Struggle to Build a Modern Defense Economy* (Ithaca, NY: Cornell University Press, 2009).

- **De-Commercialization of the PLA:** James Mulvenon, *Soldiers of Fortune: The Rise and Fall of the Chinese Military-Business Complex* (Armonk, NY: M.E. Sharpe, 2001).

APPENDIX 8: THE PLA AND THE PARTY

This appendix provides a selection of books and monographs that chart the development of the PLA since its founding on August 1, 1927. In particular, these works highlight the impact of the complex relationship between the CCP and the PLA—an issue that remains alive today.

- Monte Bullard, *China's Political-Military Evolution: The Party and the Military in the PRC, 1960–1984* (Boulder, CO: Westview Press, 1985).

- Edward L. Dreyer, *China at War, 1901–1949* (New York: Routledge, 1995).

- Harlan W. Jencks, *From Muskets to Missiles: Politics and Professionalism in the Chinese Army, 1945–1981* (Boulder, CO: Westview Press, 1982).

- Ellis Joffe, *Party and Army: Professionalism and Political Control in the Chinese Officer Corps, 1949–1964* (Cambridge, MA: Harvard East Asian Monographs, 1967).

- Ellis Joffe, *The Chinese Army after Mao* (Cambridge, MA: Harvard University Press, 1987).

- Harvey W. Nelsen, *The Chinese Military System: An Organizational Study of the Chinese People's Liberation Army* (Boulder, CO: Westview Press, 1977).

- William W. Whitson with Chen-hsia Huang, *The Chinese High Command: A History of Communist Military Politics, 1927–71* (New York: Praeger Publishers, 1973).

For a review of published analysis in the 1980s and 1990s compared to the reality of PLA modernization during the time, see, Dennis J. Blasko, "PLA Force Structure: A 20-Year Retrospective," in James Mulvenon and Andrew N.D. Yang, eds., *Seeking Truth From Facts: A Retrospective on Chinese Military Studies in the Post-Mao Era* (Santa Monica, CA: RAND, 2001), 51–86.

APPENDIX 9: CHINESE GOVERNMENT DOCUMENTS

Every two years, the State Council Information Office releases a white paper on China's national defense. Although the papers are published anonymously, the authors most often are researchers at the Academy of Military Sciences.

- *The Diversified Employment of China's Armed Forces* (2013) <http://news.xinhuanet.com/english/china/2013-04/16/c_132312681.htm>.

- *China's National Defense in 2010* <http://english.gov.cn/official/2011-03/31/content_1835499.htm>.

- *China's National Defense in 2008* <http://english.gov.cn/official/2009-01/20/content_1210227.htm>.

- *China's National Defense in 2006* <http://www.china.org.cn/english/features/book/194421.htm>.

- *China's National Defense in 2004* <http://english.gov.cn/official/2005-07/28/content_18078.htm>.

- *China's National Defense in 2002* <http://english.gov.cn/official/2005-07/28/content_17780.htm>.

- *China's National Defense in 2000* <http://english.gov.cn/official/2005-07/27/content_17524.htm>.

- *China's National Defense in 1998* <http://www.china.org.cn/e-white/5/index.htm>.

CHINESE GOVERNMENT DOCUMENTS

In the post-Mao Zedong era, the Chinese Communist Party has held its party congress much more regularly, settling into five-year cycles. At each congress, the party's general secretary presents a work report that outlines China's policy directions and objectives, including their domestic and foreign aspects. These are foundational documents that get coordinated broadly across the Chinese party-state and should be a starting point for any broad-based assessment of Beijing's policy.

- "Full Text of Hu Jintao's Report at 18th Party Congress," Xinhua, November 17, 2012
  <http://news.xinhuanet.com/english/special/18cpcnc/2012-11/17/c_131981259.htm>.

- "Full Text of Hu Jintao's Report at 17th Party Congress," Xinhua, October 24, 2007 <http://news.xinhuanet.com/english/2007-10/24/content_6938749.htm>.

- "Full Text of Jiang Zemin's Report at 16th Party Congress," Xinhua, November 18, 2002
  <http://news.xinhuanet.com/english/2002-11/18/content_633685.htm>.

The State Council Information Office also publishes other white papers describing various aspects of Chinese policy. These are published irregularly and focus on a specific topic.

- *China's Energy Policy in 2012*
  <http://www.gov.cn/english/official/2012-10/24/content_2250497.htm>.

- *China's Peaceful Development* (2011)
  <http://english.gov.cn/official/2011-09/06/content_1941354.htm>.

- *China's Space Activities in 2011*
  <http://www.gov.cn/english/official/2011-12/29/content_2033200.htm>.

- *China-Africa Economic and Trade Cooperation* (2010)
  <http://english.gov.cn/official/2010-12/23/content_1771603.htm>.

APPENDIX 9

- *The Internet in China* (2010) <http://english.gov.cn/2010-06/08/content_1622956.htm>.
- *China's Policies and Actions for Addressing Climate Change* (2008) <http://english.gov.cn/2008-10/29/content_1134544.htm>.
- *China's Space Activities in 2006* <http://www.china.org.cn/english/features/book/183672.htm>.
- *China's Peaceful Development Road* (2005) <http://www.china.org.cn/english/2005/Dec/152669.htm>.
- *China's Non-Proliferation Policy and Measures* (2003) <http://english.gov.cn/official/2005-07/28/content_17957.htm>.
- *China's Policy on Mineral Resources* (2003) <http://english.gov.cn/official/2005-07/28/content_17963.htm>.
- *The One-China Principle and the Taiwan Issue* (2000) <http://english.gov.cn/official/2005-07/27/content_17613.htm>.

APPENDIX 10: CORE CHINESE-LANGUAGE READINGS

For those with Chinese-language reading ability, the following works and suggestions are provided as a useful starting point for building one's library on the PLA. For the most part, these can be found at the National Defense University Press and Academy of Military Science bookstores in Beijing as well as the military bookstore located on the fifth floor of No. 60 on Taipei's Fuxing North Road (台北市，复兴北路，60号5楼). Some also are available for purchase online through Amazon.cn or DangDang.com. The two core works and their accompanying explanatory texts are useful starting points:

- **Academy of Military Science Strategic Research Department,** *The Science of Military Strategy,* **2013 Edition (Beijing: Academy of Military Science Press, 2013);** 军事科学院军事战略研究部，《战略学 2013 年版》(北京: 军事科学出版社).

- Shou Xiaosong, Chief Ed., *Science of Military Strategy Textbook*, 2nd Edition (Beijing: Academy of Military Science Press, 2013); 寿晓松 [编者]，《战略学教程, 第 2 版》(北京:军事科学出版社, 2013).

- **Zhang Yuliang, Chief Ed.,** *The Science of Campaigns,* **(Beijing: National Defense University Press, 2006);** 张玉良 [主编]，《战役学, 第 2 版》(北京: 国防大学出版社, 2006).

- Qiao Jie, Chief Ed., *Science of Campaigns Textbook*, 2nd Edition (Beijing: Academy of Military Science Press, 2012); 乔杰[编者]，《战役学教程,第 2 版》(北京:军事科学出版社, 2012).

- Bi Xinglin, *Campaign Theory Study Guide* (Beijing: Academy of Military Science Press, 2002); 薛兴林[编者]，《战役理论学习指南》(北京: 国防大学出版社, 2002).

APPENDIX 10

Each PLA service and branch also has a *"Science of…"* series related to campaigns, strategy, and political work, etc., as well as service-specific topics. These are more difficult to find than the PLA-wide versions and may even be classified above internal or military use only. From time to time, however, copies, such as *The Science of Second Artillery Campaigns*, make it outside China and Taiwanese presses make them available for purchase. Additionally, they each publish an officers' handbook (军官手册) and enlisted force handbook (士兵手册).

The Academy of Military Science also publishes a course materials (教程) series entitled "Academy of Military Science Graduate Textbook Series" (军事科学院硕士研究生系列教材). Apart from the two identified above, the volumes cover a wide range of topics from national defense construction (国防建设) and non-combat military operations (非战争军事运动) to legal affairs (军事法制) and political work (军队政治工作). These books are starting points that explain PLA terminology and concepts as well as the underlying thinking for Chinese officers and analysts of military affairs.

Two encyclopedia series provide useful reference guides to history and terminology used within the PLA and its constituent services and branch. The first is Chinese Military Encyclopedia Volumes (中国军事百科全书学科分册), which provide overviews of functional military topics, such as informatization and logistics. These are published by the Encyclopedia of China Publishing House (中国大百科全书出版社). The second includes the service-focused encyclopedias published by affiliated publishing houses, such as the *Chinese Air Force Encyclopedia* (中国空军百科全书) published by Aviation Industry Press (航空工业出版社) and the *Chinese Navy Encyclopedia* (中国海军百科全书) published by Haichao Press (海潮出版社).

Finally, every Chinese leader from Mao Zedong onward has several volumes related to their military thought as well as guidance for military operations and modernization. These include a volume for each of the PLA's different elements. For Hu Jintao's contributions, look for titles including his "Scientific Development Concept" (科学发展观). For secondary texts that summarize the pertinent details, the Academy of

[124]

Military Science Graduate Textbook Series also contains entries on leadership thinking about military affairs.

The PLA's individual elements and military regions also publish newspapers. Although these are not publicly available, these newspapers and other internal periodicals can be found in Taiwan at places like the Mainland Affairs Council library and, for older items, the Institute for International Relations at National Cheng-chi University. Apart from the aforementioned *People's Liberation Army Daily* (解放军报), official PLA news outlets include the following:

- PLA Navy: *People's Navy* (人民海军)
- PLA Air Force: *Air Force News* (空军报)
- Second Artillery: *Rocket Force News* (火箭兵报)
- Beijing MR: Comrades-in-Arms News (战友报)
- Chengdu MR: *Battle Flag News* (战其报)
- Guangzhou MR: *Soldiers News* (战士报)
- Jinan MR: *Vanguard News* (前卫报)
- Lanzhou MR: *People's Armed Forces* (人民军队)
- Nanjing MR: *People's Front* (人民前线)
- Shenyang MR: *Advance News* (前进报)

APPENDIX 11: WORKS REVIEWED (IN ORDER)

- Dennis J. Blasko, *The Chinese Army Today: Tradition and Transformation for the 21st Century*, 2nd Edition (New York: Routledge, 2012).

- Paul H.B. Godwin and Alice L. Miller, *China's Forbearance Has Limits: Chinese Threat and Retaliation Signaling and Its Implications for a Sino-American Military Confrontation*, China Strategic Perspectives, No. 6 (Washington, DC: National Defense University Institute for National Strategic Studies, 2013).

- Bernard D. Cole, *The Great Wall at Sea: China's Navy Enters the Twenty-First Century*, 2nd Edition (Annapolis, MD: Naval Institute Press, 2012).

- Kevin Pollpeter and Kenneth Allen, eds., *PLA as Organization v2.0* (Vienna, VA: Defense Group Inc., Forthcoming 2015).

- Andrew Scobell, David Lai, and Roy Kamphausen, eds., *Chinese Lessons from Other Peoples' War* (Carlisle, PA: Army War College Strategic Studies Institute, 2011).

- Roy Kamphausen, David Lai, and Travis Tanner, eds., *Assessing the People's Liberation Army in the Hu Jintao Era* (Carlisle, PA: Army War College Strategic Studies Institute, 2014).

- Andrew S. Erickson and Lyle J. Goldstein, eds., *Chinese Aerospace Power: Evolving Maritime Roles* (Annapolis, MD: Naval Institute Press with the China Maritime Studies Institute, 2011).

- Richard P. Hallion, Roger Cliff, and Phillip C. Saunders, eds., *The Chinese Air Force: Evolving Concepts, Roles, and Capabilities* (Washington, DC: National Defense University, Institute for National Strategic Studies, 2012).

- Ashley J. Tellis and Travis Tanner, eds., *Strategic Asia 2012–13: China's Military Challenge* (Seattle, WA: The National Bureau of Asian Research, 2012).

WORKS REVIEWED

- Ashley J. Tellis, Abraham M. Denmark, and Travis Tanner, eds., *Strategic Asia 2013–14: Asia in the Second Nuclear Age* (Seattle, WA: The National Bureau of Asian Research, 2013).

- Tai Ming Cheung, *Fortifying China: The Struggle to Build a Modern Defense Economy* (Ithaca, NY: Cornell University Press, 2009).

- William C. Hannas, James Mulvenon, and Anna B. Puglisi, *Chinese Industrial Espionage: Technology Acquisition and Military Modernization* (New York: Routledge, 2013).

- Mikhail Barabanov, Vasiliy Kashin, and Konstantin Makienko, *Shooting Star: China's Military Machine in the 21st Century* (Minneapolis, MN: East View Press, 2012).

- Larry M. Wortzel, *The Dragon Extends Its Reach: Chinese Military Power Goes Global* (Herndon, VA: Potomac Books Inc., 2013).

- Andrew Chubb, "Propaganda, Not Policy: Explaining the PLA's 'Hawkish Faction' (Part One)," *Jamestown Foundation China Brief*, Vol. 13, No. 15 (July 2013); "Propaganda as Policy? Explaining the PLA's 'Hawkish Faction' (Part Two)," *Jamestown Foundation China Brief*, Vol. 13, No. 16 (August 2013).

- Mark Stokes and Russell Hsiao, *The People's Liberation Army General Political Department: Political Warfare with Chinese Characteristics*, Occasional Paper, Project 2049 Institute (October 2013).

INDEX

Academy of Military Science 11, 13, 26, 120, 123–124

Active Defense 31, 86–87

aerial refueling 28, 41

Ahrens, Nathaniel 50n

air defense 15, 39, 43, 45, 55

Air Defense Identification Zone (ADIZ) 12, 39

air force (see People's Liberation Army Air Force)

aircraft carrier 36, 39, 47, 91

Alderman, Daniel 88, 105

Allen, Kenneth 7, 16–17, 24, 36, 41n, 42–44, 45n, 72, 91–92, 100, 126

amphibious assault 28

analyzing foreign militaries 4–5, 74–77

    Bibliography 85

anti-submarine warfare 38, 55

Anderson, Eric 111

Andrew, Martin, 92, 98

Annual PLA Conference 22–36, 37, 43, 111–113

Anti-Access/Area-Denial 25, 31, 39, 67, 89

anti-satellite (ASAT) 41, 67n, 110–111

anti-ship ballistic missile 28, 40–41, 66, 76, 118

anti-ship missiles 39, 55

Army Day 76

ASBM (see anti-ship ballistic missile)

Ayuso, Wanda 23n, 36

Bakos, George 90, 109

ballistic missile 25, 27n, 30, 38, 40–41, 45, 47, 66–67, 71, 76, 102–103, 113, 118

Barabanov, Mikhail 47, 106, 127

Becker, Jeffrey 91, 101

Berkowitz, Samuel 32n, 88, 98

Bi Xinglin 123

Bibliographies

    1990s Revolution in the PLA 118

    Analyzing Foreign Militaries 85

INDEX

Bibliographies, con't.
  Annual PLA Conference 111–113
  CAPS-RAND Conference 114–115
  China Maritime Studies Institute Volumes 113–114
  China today and tomorrow 84
  China's Political System 83
  China-Taiwan Military Balance 107–108
  Chinese Government Documents 120–122
  civil-military relations (party-army relations) 104–105, 119
  Congressional Research Service Reports 117
  Cyber, Information Operations, and Intelligence 108–110
  Defense-Industrial Base 106–107
  National Security and Foreign Policymaking 96–98
  Nuclear Forces 103–104
  organizational basics 100
  People's Liberation Army – General 98–99
  PLA Air Force 100–101
  PLA and the Party 119
  PLA Ground Forces 100
  PLA Navy 101–102

Bibliographies, con't.
  Second Artillery 102–103
  Space Issues and Space-based Capabilities 110–111
  Strategic Asia 115–117
  U.S.-China relations 83
  Understanding China 83–84
Bickford, Thomas 92
Bishop, Bill 81–82
Bitzinger, Richard 92, 106
Blasko, Dennis 4n, 7–9, 15–17, 23n, 32n, 41, 65, 68, 72, 88, 92, 98, 100, 118 119, 126
Blumenthal, Dan 64, 92
Brady, Anne-Marie 63n
Bueschel, Richard 43n, 101
Bullard, Monte 119
Burkitt, Laurie 25, 30n, 113
Burles, Mark 96
Bush, Richard 107

C4I (see Command, Control, Communications, Computers, Intelligence)
C4ISR (see Command, Control, Communications, Computers, Intelligence, Surveillance and Reconnaissance)
CAPS-RAND Conference 42–46, 114–115

[129]

INDEX

Central Military Commission (CMC) 9n, 11, 13, 17–19, 30–32, 44, 82, 86, 87, 91

CETC (see China Electronics Technology Group Corporation)

Chaffin, Greg 115

Chang, Amy 75n, 108

Chase, Michael 2n, 32n, 36, 67n, 88, 92, 98, 102–103

Chechnya 25, 29

Chen Jian 96

Chen, David 36n, 91

Cheng Ta-chen 103

Cheng, Dean 17, 20–21, 25–27, 30, 92, 107, 110, 118

Cheung, Tai Ming 32n, 47–51, 56n, 88, 92, 98, 106, 109, 118, 127

China Brief (see *Jamestown Foundation China Brief*)

China Central Television (CCTV) 59–60

China Electronic Technology Group Corporation 88

China Leadership Monitor 33n, 79

China Maritime Studies Institute 37, 67n, 79, 113–114, 126

China National Knowledge Infrastructure (CNKI) 38–39, 54

China Brief (see *Jamestown Foundation China Brief*)

China SignPost 41n, 81

China Strategic Perspectives 7, 79

China Vitae leadership database 80

China's National Defense white paper 5–6, 28, 41, 65, 70, 76, 88, 120

Chinese Communist Party (CCP) 4, 12, 17–18, 27, 30–34, 44, 58–61, 82–83, 86, 104, 119, 121

Christensen, Thomas 5, 64, 92, 96, 103

Christman, Ron 25, 67n, 92, 102

Chubb, Andrew 57, 59–61, 82, 127

civil-military relations 4, 31–32, 79, 119

Bibliography 104–105

Cliff, Roger 37, 47n, 89–90, 92, 106–107, 114, 126

CMC (see Central Military Commission)

CNKI (see China National Knowledge Infrastructure)

coast guard 15

Cole, Bernard (Bud) 7, 14–16, 72, 92, 101, 126

Cole, J. Michael 92

Collins, Gabriel (Gabe) 41, 114

[130]

INDEX

command and control 21n, 46, 68

command, control, communications, and intelligence (C4I) 20

command, control, communications, computers, intelligence, surveillance and reconnaissance (C4ISR) 38, 58, 65, 67, 90

Congressional Research Service 6, 94, 96, 117

Corbett, John 17, 23n, 24, 30n, 72, 93

counterinsurgency 25, 29

counter-intervention (*fanganshe*) 67

Crane, Keith 47n, 107

Crawford, Lisa 88

cruise missiles 38, 47, 102–103

cyber 6, 10n, 32, 54, 67–68, 90, 106

   Bibliography 108–110

Dai Qingmin 10n, 90

Dai Xu 59–60

Deal, Jacqueline 93

defense industry 16, 24, 45, 46–56, 106–107, 118

   Bibliography 106–107

defense white paper (see *China's National Defense*)

Deng Xiaoping 4, 49, 65

Denmark, Abraham 103, 115–116, 127

deterrence 45, 61, 67, 70, 102–103, 108, 110

DF-21D (see anti-ship ballistic missile)

DH-10 long-rang land attack cruise missile 28, 66

Ding, Arthur 93

Dockham, John 3n

doctrine, 15, 20–24, 31, 36, 42–44, 46, 58, 67n, 89, 99, 109

Dotson, John 75n

Downs, Chuck 108

Dreyer, Edward 119

Dreyer, June Teufel 83

dual-use 48–50, 118

Durnin, Matthew 110

Dutton, Peter 39

early-warning aircraft 38

East China Sea 12, 39, 59, 61n

Eastern Arsenal blog 81

Easton, Ian 68n, 93, 104, 107, 110

electronic warfare 10n, 26, 38–39, 43, 47, 58, 67–68, 90

Elleman, Bruce 96

Ellings, Richard 116–117

[131]

INDEX

Engstrom, Jeffrey 32n, 88, 98

Erickson, Andrew 28n, 37, 40–41, 65–67, 76n, 81–82, 93, 99, 101–103, 113–114, 118, 126

escalation 24, 37, 67n, 96, 108

espionage 47, 51–54, 56, 90, 106, 109, 127 (see also intelligence)

exercises 9, 23, 36, 82

expeditionary warfare 27–28, 31

Falklands War 25, 27

falü zhan (see legal warfare)

fanganshe (see counter-intervention)

Fan Yang 111

Farley, Robert, 53n

Fei, John 101

Feigenbaum, Evan 50, 106

Fenby, Jonathan 84

fighter aircraft 44, 54n, 47, 66

Finkelstein, David 13–14, 21n, 24, 26n, 40, 72, 93, 97, 99, 104

Fisher, Richard 41, 76, 93

Flanagan, Stephen 98

four general departments (*si zongbu*) 13, 17, 44, 61

Four Mechanisms (*si ge jizhi*) 50

Fravel, M. Taylor 5, 67n, 82, 93, 96, 98, 103,

Friedberg, Aaron 93, 116–117

Gao Xiaoxing 102

Garafola, Cristina 35n

Garnaut, John 39n

Gates, Robert 71n

General Armament Department 13n, 19

General Logistics Department 13n, 19

General Political Department 13n, 19, 31, 57–58, 61, 127

General Staff Department 11, 13n, 19, 35, 44, 46, 90

Gertz, Bill 71n

Giarra, Paul 41

Gill, Bates 11n, 35n

Glosny, Michael 2n, 93, 107

Godwin, Paul 7, 11–13, 16, 87, 93, 96, 106, 126

Goldstein, Lyle 2n, 27n, 37, 55n, 67n, 93, 101, 113–114, 126

Gormley, Dennis 103

governing party (*zhizhengdang*) 33–34, 83

GPD/LO (see Liaison Department)

ground forces (see People's Liberation Army Ground Forces)

Gulf of Aden 28n

INDEX

Gulf War 20n, 25–27, 50n, 53n, 118

Gunness, Kristen 32n, 88, 93, 98, 104

Hagen, Jeff 101

Hagt, Eric 24, 41, 110–111

Hague, Elizabeth 24, 101

Hallion, Richard 37, 89–90, 101, 114, 126

Hannas, William 47, 52, 106, 109, 127

Harold, Scott, 32n, 88, 93, 98, 107, 114

Hartnett, Daniel 31–33, 86, 93

hawks 57, 59–61, 127

Heath, Timothy 2n, 32–34, 83, 93, 97, 104

Hekler, Garth 38–39

Heginbotham, Eric 101

helicopters 38, 41, 66

Henley, Lonnie 17, 23–24, 36, 93

Herman, Michael 85

Heuser, Beatrice 85

Holmes, James 75n, 102

Hong Kong 7, 48

Hsiao, L.C. Russell 57, 61–62, 127

Hu Jintao 22–23, 30–33, 35–36, 76, 86–87, 89, 105, 111, 121, 124, 126

Huang Chen-hsia 105, 119

Huawei 50

Hughes, Christopher 64

information operations 6, 8, 10n, 26, 58, 68n, 90, 108–110

information warfare 57–58, 90, 109–110

informatization (*xinxihua*) 34–36, 65, 124

informatized conditions 32, 34, 46, 87, 89

Inkster, Nigel 109

Integrated Air and Space [Aerospace] Operations (*kongtian yiti*) 89–90

Integrated Joint Operations 89

Integrated Network Electronic Warfare (*wangdian yitizhan*) 58, 90

intelligence 3n, 6, 11, 16, 18, 27, 29, 36, 38, 41, 51–54, 62, 67–68, 71n, 85

Bibliography 108–110

internal security 24, 37, 54n, 65, 118

Jamestown Foundation China Brief 9n, 13n, 21n, 32n, 34–36, 41n, 55n, 57, 79, 88–89, 91, 127

Jencks, Harlan 4, 13n, 30n, 93, 105, 119

[133]

INDEX

Jiang Zemin 45, 47, 49, 121

Joffe, Ellis, 4, 105, 119

Johnston, Alastair Iain, 5, 97, 103

joint operations 20–21, 89

joint task force 36n, 91

junmin ronghe (see military-civil integration)

Kamphausen, Roy 20–24, 26n, 65, 86, 89, 93, 104–105, 109, 111–112, 118, 126

Kan, Shirley 117

Karber, Phillip 69

Kashin, Vasiliy 47, 106, 127

Keck, Zachary 54n

Kivlehan-Wise, Maryanne 94

Klapakis, Philip 23n

kongtian yiti (see Integrated Air and Space [Aerospace] Operations)

Kostecka, Daniel 94

Krekel, Bryan 90, 109

Krepon, Michael 110–111

Krumel, Glenn 100

Kiselycznyk, Michael 105

Kulacki, Gregory 69n

Kuo, Mercy 116

Lafferty, Brian 88

Lai, David 20n, 22–24, 86, 89, 94, 104–105, 109, 111–112, 118, 126

Lampton, David (Mike) 97

Lane, Dennison 113

Lanzit, Kevin 94

lawfare (see legal warfare)

Lawrence, Susan 83, 117

legal warfare (*falü zhan*) 26–27, 39n, 58

Lewis, Jeffrey 64, 68–70, 103

Lewis, John 97, 104

Li Nan 36, 105, 113

Li Xiaobing 100

Liaison Department of the General Political Department (GPD/LO) 61–63

liaison work (*lianluo gongzuo*) 61

liang ge buxiang shiying (see Two Incompatibles)

lianluo gongzuo (see liaison work)

Liebenberg, David 91, 101

Lieberthal, Kenneth 64, 83

Liff, Adam 99

Lilley, James 108

Lin, Jeffrey 81

Lin, Jenny 109

Lindsay, Jon 109

Liu Yawei 59n, 105

[134]

INDEX

Liu, Dimon 113

logistics 13–14, 18, 26, 28, 74, 124

Lord, Carnes 114

Lu Ning 97

Luce, Matthew 88

Luo Yuan 59–60

Luttwak, Edward 85

Ma, Damien 84

Mackenzie, Peter, 91, 101

Mahan, Alfred Thayer 75, 102

Mahnken, Thomas 85, 94

Makienko, Konstantin 47, 106, 127

Mann, James 83

Mao Zedong 4, 8, 42n, 48, 70, 98–99, 105, 115, 119, 121, 124

Marble, Andrew 116

Marti, Michael 98

Mastro, Oriana Skylar 5, 94, 108

Mattis, Peter 51n, 109

May, Ernest 85

McCauley, Kevin 21, 35n, 89, 94

McClung, Sean 40

McDevitt, Michael 14n, 94, 97

McGauvran, Michael 41

McGregor, Richard 83

McReynolds, Joe 11n, 34–35, 99

Medeiros, Evan 47n, 103, 107–108

media warfare (see public opinion warfare)

military regions, 13, 17, 19, 29, 44, 46, 125

military theory (*junshi lilun*) 20

military unit cover designator (MUCD) 66, 77

military-civil integration (*junmin ronghe*) 88

military-to-military diplomacy 36–37, 82

Miller, Alice 7, 11, 13, 16, 79, 87, 96, 126

Miller, Frank 94

Millett, Allan 74n, 85

Ministry of National Defense (Japan) 80

Ministry of National Defense (PRC) 18, 82, 86

Ministry of National Defense (ROC, Taiwan) 42, 82, 108

Minnick, Wendell 54n, 94

Mirsky, Jonathan 30n

Morrison, Wayne 117

Mulvenon, James 4n, 11n, 13n, 16–17, 24, 30n, 33–35, 42n, 47n, 51–52, 61n, 72n, 94, 99, 100, 106–107, 109, 115, 118–119, 127

Murray, William 94, 101, 107, 114

[135]

INDEX

Murray, Williamson 74n, 85

Muth, Jorg, 85

Nathan, Andrew 97

National Air and Space Intelligence Center (NASIC) 4n, 8n, 18n, 100–103

National Defense Student Program 41

National Defense University (PRC) 13, 26, 123

National Defense University (U.S.) 7, 11, 20n, 27, 37, 42, 79, 87, 90–90, 94–98, 101–104, 108, 114, 126

National Institute of Defense Studies (NIDS, Japan) 80, 95

National People's Congress 76, 82

navy (see People's Liberation Army Navy)

Nelsen, Harvey 4, 119

neutron bomb 104

New Historic Missions (*xin de lishi shiming*) 31–33, 65, 76, 86

newspapers 10, 12, 26n, 54, 72, 125

NIDS (see National Institute of Defense Studies)

nuclear 6, 19, 61, 80, 106, 115
  Bibliography 103–104

nuclear, con't.
  no first use 68, 70
  policy 68, 70
  weapons 48, 64, 68–71

O'Dowd, Edward 30n, 72, 94, 99

O'Hanlon, Michael 107–108

O'Rourke, Ronald 94, 117

Office of Naval Intelligence 4n, 8n, 15n, 18, 91, 94, 100, 102

officer grade and rank 17, 35–36, 90–91

Ohlandt, Chad 106

organizational basics bibliography 100

Orletsky, David 108

Osnos, Evan 84

Pacific Command (U.S.) 25, 32, 71n, 95

Pan, Philip 84

PAP (see People's Armed Police)

Party Congress 24–25, 33–34, 113, 121

party-army relations (see civil-military relations)

Peng Guangqian 11, 87

People's Armed Police (PAP) 17, 19, 23n, 29, 65, 118

People's Liberation Army (PLA)

INDEX

Bibliography (General) 98–99

Air Force (PLAAF) 6, 13, 18–20, 35, 37, 40–46, 58, 66, 68, 89–90, 101, 114, 124–126
  Bibliography 100–101

People's Liberation Army, con't.

  Ground Forces 6, 8, 13, 19, 30n, 35, 44, 58, 65, 68
    Bibliography 100

  Navy (PLAN) 6, 8n 13–16, 18–20, 35–36, 41–42, 44, 58, 65–66, 68, 76, 79–80, 90, 91, 100–102, 114, 117, 124–125
    Bibliography 101–102

Persian Gulf War (see Gulf War)

Pillsbury, Michael 94, 97, 111

PLA (see People's Liberation Army)

PLAAF (see People's Liberation Army Air Force)

PLAN (see People's Liberation Army Navy)

political commissar 13n, 19, 33, 44, 61

political warfare 27, 41, 57–63, 80, 127

Pollack, Jonathan 100, 115

Pollpeter, Kevin 4n, 7, 67, 90–91, 94, 100, 107, 111, 126

Pomfret, John 71n

Porter, Patrick 85

power projection 65–66

precision strike 20, 43, 107

Project 2049 Institute 57, 61, 68n, 80–81, 93, 95, 104, 107, 109–110, 127

propaganda 5, 13, 41, 57–63, 75, 127

psychological warfare (*xinli zhan*) 26n, 58, 62

public opinion warfare (*yulun zhan*) 26n, 58

Puglisi, Anna 47, 52, 106, 109, 127

Puska, Susan 13n, 32n, 72, 88, 94, 98

Qiao Jie 123

Qiao Liang 10

RAND 4n, 17, 32, 42, 45–47, 72n, 88, 92–101, 105–108, 114–115, 119

Ratner, Ely 2n

Ray, Jonathan, 104

Reid, Toy 108

Ren, Justine Zheng 59n, 105

Reveron, Derek 109

rocket forces (see Second Artillery)

Ross, Robert 2n, 108

Ryan, Mark 14n, 97

[137]

INDEX

Sahgal, Arun 64

satellites 41, 48, 67–68

Saunders, Phillip 2n, 37, 42n, 79, 89–90, 94, 101–102, 105, 107, 114, 126

Science of Campaigns (*zhanyi xue*) 8–9, 123

Science of Military Strategy (*zhanlüe xue*) 8–11, 62, 75, 87, 123

Scobell, Andrew 20–26, 30n, 94, 97, 105, 109, 112–113, 118, 126

Second Artillery 6, 13, 19, 35–36, 41, 43, 66–68, 89, 124–125

    Bibliography 102–103

Segal, Gerald 98, 107

Shambaugh, David 20n, 63–64, 71–72, 95, 99, 108

Shearer, Andrew 64

Shen Dingli 111

shipbuilding 15, 55

Shirk, Susan 13n

Shlapak, David 45–46, 95, 108

Shou Xiaosong 123

Shraberg, Aaron 88, 91

Shulsky, Abram 96

si zongbu (see four general departments)

signals intelligence 52, 81, 109

Sino-American relations (see U.S.-China relations)

Solin, Gail 3n

South China Sea 14, 59, 61n

South Sea Conversations 59n

Soviet Union 9, 14, 47–48, 51n, 54, 65, 90

space 4n, 6, 8n, 18–19, 29, 32, 45, 48, 58, 67, 89–90, 100–102, 121–122

    Bibliography 110–111

State Council Information Office 120–121

Stillion, John 101

Stokes, Mark 57, 61–63, 66–68, 72, 89, 95, 103–104, 109–110, 127

Strange, Austin 28n

Strategic Asia 58, 64–71, 77, 99, 103, 115–117, 126–127

submarine 14, 38, 90, 101, 107

Suettinger, Robert 83

Sun Tzu 8, 62, 73

Suttmeier, Richard 51n

Swaine, Michael 42n, 95, 97, 102, 105, 108, 114

system of systems operations 35n, 89

Tanner, Murray Scot 24, 44, 95, 108

[138]

INDEX

Tanner, Travis 22–24, 64, 86, 89, 99, 103–104, 111–112, 115–116, 118, 126–127

Taiwan Security Research 81

Taiwan Strait 14, 27, 45, 50n, 82, 112, 118

   China-Taiwan Military Balance Bibliography 107–108

Tellis, Ashley 64, 71n, 99, 103, 111, 115–116, 126–127

Thomas, Timothy 68n, 90, 110

Thompson, Julia 110

Three Provides and One Role (*san ge tigong, yi ge fahui*) (see New Historic Missions)

san ge tigong, yi ge fahui (see New Historic Missions)

Three Warfares (*san zhong zhanzheng, sanzhan*) 26, 58–59, 61–62

Two Incompatibles (*liang ge buxiang shiying*) 9n, 32, 87–88

Twomey, Christopher 30, 67n, 89, 95

training 8, 23–24, 29, 35–37, 41n, 43–45, 52, 62, 67n, 85, 104, 112, 118

territorial disputes 15, 28 32, 71, 96

U.S.-China relations 5, 82–83, 103, 108, 117

U.S.-China relations, con't.
   Bibliography 83

U.S.-China Security and Economic Commission (USCC) 32n, 75n–76n, 88, 90, 95, 98, 109–111

Ulman, Wayne 95

Understanding China Bibliography 83–84

United Front Work Department 12, 59

USCC (see U.S.-China Security and Economic Commission)

USSR (see Soviet Union)

Van Riper, Paul 74n

Vietnam 25, 30, 87

Wan, William 69n

wangdian yitizhan (see Integrated Network Electronic Warfare)

Wasserstrom, Jeffrey 84

Watman, Kenneth 74n

Weisenbloom, Mark 113

white paper, defense (see *China's National Defense*)

White, Timothy 41

Whiting, Allen 98

Whitson, William 4, 105, 119

Willner, Albert 95

[139]

INDEX

Wills, Michael 71n, 116

Wilson, Andrew 101

Wilson, Barry 108

Wilson, James 85

Wilson, Jordan 111

Wise, David 54n

Wolfers, Arnold 85

Wortzel, Larry 10n, 13n, 24–25, 30n, 57–59, 61, 95, 104, 112–113, 127

Wu Riqiang 104

Wang Xiangsui 10

Xi Jinping 32, 34n

xinxihua (see informatization)

xinli zhan (see psychological warfare)

Xue Litai 97, 104

Xinhua 4, 12, 21, 65, 75, 80, 120–121

Yamaguchi, Shinji 95

Yang Hui 29

Yang, Andrew Nien-Dzu 4n, 13–14, 17n, 42, 61n, 72n, 99–100, 102, 108, 114–115, 119

Yang, David 106

Yang, Philip 81

Yang, Richard 42n, 107, 115

Yao Youzhi 11n, 87

Yao Yunzhu 99

Yeaw, Christopher 103

Yoshihara, Toshi 75n, 95, 102

You Ji 93, 105

Yu Bin 29

Yuan Jingdong 95, 103

yulun zhan (see public opinion warfare)

Yung, Christopher 27–28, 42n, 95, 102, 114

Zhang Xiaoming 30n, 40, 95, 101

Zhang Yuliang 123

Zhang Zhaozhong 59

zhanlüe xue (see *Science of Military Strategy*)

zhanyi xue (see *Science of Campaigns*)

zhiwu dengji (see officer grade and rank)

zhizhengdang (see governing party)

Acknowledgements

The author would like to thank Richard Valcourt, whose original request for a review essay generated this primer and who continued to solicit my writing despite my failure to turn in a manuscript, and Peter Wood, whose comments on an early draft encouraged me to go beyond *The Chinese Army Today*, *Chinese Aerospace Power*, and *The Great Wall at Sea*. Participants in the University of Cambridge reading group on Chinese foreign and security policy (2014) helped identify what belonged here. *Defense News*' Wendell Minnick graciously loaned me several books necessary for completing the project and helped with indexing. Ken Allen, Jonathan Acuff, James Barker, Dennis Blasko, Michael Chase, John Corbett, Ian Easton, Anne Elizabeth, Andrew Erickson, Taylor Fravel, Samantha Hoffman, Isaac Kardon, Oriana Skylar Mastro, Nathan Mattis, Wendell Minnick, Robert Suettinger, Dan Tobin, Chris Tran, and Cynthia Watson offered useful comments, corrections, and additions for which I am grateful. Any mistakes are my own and remain despite their best efforts. Finally, I also would like to thank Ken Allen, Dennis Blasko, and Roy Kamphausen, who over the years have offered valuable counsel and served as generous mentors (as they have for so many others), and without whom this essay could not have been written.

About the Author

Peter Mattis is a Fellow in the China Program at The Jamestown Foundation, where he also edited the biweekly electronic journal, *China Brief*, from 2011 to 2013. For 2014–2015, he was a visiting fellow at the Institute of International Relations at National Cheng-chi University. Mr. Mattis earned his M.A. in Security Studies from Georgetown University, and B.A.s in Political Science and Asian Studies from the University of Washington. He previously worked as an international affairs analyst for the U.S. Government and as a research associate at the National Bureau of Asian Research. He can be reached by email <mattis@jamestown.org>.

Made in the USA
Monee, IL
19 December 2019